THE NEW BIBLE CURE FOR DEPRESSION & ANXIETY

DON COLBERT, MD

SILOAM

Most CHARISMA HOUSE BOOK GROUP products are available at special quantity discounts for bulk purchase for sales promotions, premiums, fund-raising, and educational needs. For details, write Charisma House Book Group, 600 Rinehart Road, Lake Mary, Florida 32746, or telephone (407) 333-0600.

THE NEW BIBLE CURE FOR DEPRESSION AND ANXIETY
  by Don Colbert, MD
Published by Siloam; Charisma Media/Charisma House Book Group
600 Rinehart Road; Lake Mary, Florida 32746
www.charismahouse.com

Design Director: Bill Johnson; cover design by Amanda Potter

Copyright © 2009 by Don Colbert, MD
All rights reserved

Library of Congress Cataloging in Publication

Colbert, Don.
  The new Bible cure for depression and anxiety / Don Colbert.
    p. cm.
  Includes bibliographical references (p.   ) and index.
  ISBN 978-1-59979-760-1

1. Depression, Mental--Religious aspects--Christianity. 2. Anxiety--Religious aspects--Christianity. I. Title.
    RC537.C6335 2009
    616.85'27--dc22

                                                    2009029220

E-book ISBN: 978-1-61638-016-8

CONTENTS

A BRAND-NEW BIBLE CURE
FOR A BRAND-NEW YOU!

T HE SECRET IS out—*even Christians get depressed.* Unfortunately, Christian people often feel that they must hide their pain and pretend that nothing is wrong. This act in itself can make their condition much worse and more difficult to overcome. If you are battling with depression or anxiety, or if someone in your family is suffering from depression or anxiety, I can confidently tell you that there is hope.

Before I go any further, it is important that I make the following statement: If you or a loved one are having any suicidal thoughts or thoughts of harming yourself or others in any way, it is critically important that you consult your primary care physician or go to the nearest emergency room. Thoughts such as these mean that you are suffering from severe depression, and you will probably need special attention in order to control the severity of your symptoms.

However, for the majority of people, the concepts outlined in this book will help you to overcome both depression and anxiety without the use of medications. You or a loved one may feel depressed or anxious at the moment, but you took an important first step toward complete healing, health, and joy when you picked up this book. As a caring Christian and as a medical doctor, I wrote this book specifically to help you and those you love take

1

hold of what Jesus called "inexpressible joy." (This must surely be the opposite of depression, an "inexpressible sadness.")

The apostle Peter said that this kind of joy stems from our love for Jesus Christ: "You love him even though you have never seen him. Though you do not see him now, you trust him; and you rejoice with a glorious, inexpressible joy" (1 Pet. 1:8).

This Bible Cure book will help you move from depression to happiness and from anxiety to peace of mind. Welcome to yet another hope-filled book in the Bible Cure series to help you know how to keep the temple of your body fit and healthy emotionally and mentally. In this series of books, you will uncover God's divine plan of health for body, soul, and spirit through modern medicine, good nutrition, and the medicinal power of Scripture and prayer.

Originally published as *The Bible Cure for Depression and Anxiety* in 1999, *The New Bible Cure for Depression and Anxiety* has been revised and updated with the latest medical research on depression and anxiety. If you compare it side by side with the previous edition, you'll see that it's also larger, allowing me to expand greatly upon the information provided in the previous edition and provide you with a deeper understanding of what you face and how to overcome it.

Unchanged from the previous edition are the timeless, life-changing, and healing scriptures throughout this book that will strengthen and encourage your spirit and soul. The proven principles, truths, and guidelines in these passages anchor the practical and medical insights also contained in this book. They will effectively focus your prayers, thoughts, and actions so you can step into God's plan of divine health for you—a plan that includes victory over depression and anxiety.

Another change since the original *The Bible Cure for Depression and Anxiety* was published is that I've released a foundational book,

The Seven Pillars of Health. I encourage you to read it because the principles of health it contains are the foundation to healthy living that will affect all areas of your life. It sets the stage for everything you will ever read in any other book I've published—including this one.

I pray that these spiritual and practical suggestions for health, nutrition, and fitness will bring wholeness to your life, increase your spiritual understanding, and strengthen your ability to worship and serve God.

—Don Colbert, MD

A **BIBLE CURE** Prayer for You

Heavenly Father, I ask in the name of Jesus that You would open my heart and mind to the truth and absolute power of Your Word, the Bible. Give me supernatural hope and total assurance that if I come to You with my burdens, then You can and will help me totally overcome depression. Give me the courage and the ability to apply everything I learn to my own life so I can live in complete victory over fear, anxiety, and worry. Thank You, Father. I give You all of the glory and praise for my healing and victory, in the name of my healer, Jesus Christ. Amen.

JOY INSTEAD OF SADNESS

L ET ME GET right to the point: If you feel depressed at this very moment, *you don't have to stay depressed.* Take courage, because *The New Bible Cure for Depression and Anxiety* will give you positive natural and spiritual steps to help you overcome depression, sadness, anxiety, and worry. You can start this very minute to move from the "pit of pain" to the plain of stability, wholeness, and peace of mind.

As a practicing medical doctor for more than twenty-five years, I have seen a dramatic rise in both depression and anxiety in my patients. The statistics on mental health disorders are absolutely staggering in the United States. It is estimated that in any given year 26.2 percent of adult Americans—about one in every four people—suffer from a diagnosable mental disorder.[1] This figure translates to approximately 57.7 million people.[2]

Americans are also typically stressed to the maximum—and the stress level is increasing. I believe Americans are experiencing significantly more stress now than they were when I published the first edition of this book in 1999. Today's newspapers and twenty-four-hour news networks often report news—such as threats of war and terrorism—that provoke people to become depressed and anxious.

And what many Americans are experiencing firsthand is even more stressful than what they see on the news. Due to the downward spiral in the economy, many Americans are losing their jobs, losing their homes to foreclosure, or they have lost a large amount of their savings in the stock market. Many people who still have jobs are working longer and harder at the same jobs—some for less pay and with less employee benefits.

Then there is family stress—not having enough hours in the day to get everything done. Also, many families have been broken through divorce or blended together through remarriage, creating even more stress. Many teens are rebelling or abusing drugs. Even children worry about things they used to never have to worry about, such as gang violence, school shootings, and child abductions.

Situations like these can cause even the most optimistic of us to become stressed, anxious, worried, fearful, or a little down. But for some, these feelings don't quickly pass; instead they linger and turn into depression and anxiety.

Depression and anxiety can lead to severe emotional pain along with physical symptoms, destroyed marriages and relationships, substance abuse, or loss of employment as a result of habitual absences. Depression and anxiety can take over to the point that they prevent you from living a productive and fulfilling life. If this describes you or someone you love, it is likely the result of either depression or anxiety—or both. I will address anxiety in the next chapter. For now, let's focus on depression.

As I said, it is normal for people to feel "down" or to have the "blues" when they experience a sad circumstance such as the death of a loved one or friend, the loss of a job, a divorce, separation, or some other significant loss. However, anyone who experiences continued depression without any recognizable cause should know that this may be a warning sign of major depression, an affliction that affects millions of people around the world.

The good news is that you can overcome these conditions. God has provided you with resources in both the natural and spiritual realms to defeat depression and anxiety. As you take the positive steps outlined in this book, hope should begin to replace depression and inner peace will overcome anxiety. (Note: If your depression persists or deepens, consult a physician, pastor, psychologist, mental health counselor, or Christian counselor. At times even the strongest ones among us need a helping hand to climb over an obstacle.)

> Don't worry about anything; instead, pray about everything. Tell God what you need, and thank him for all he has done. Then you will experience God's peace, which exceeds anything we can understand. His peace will guard your hearts and minds as you live in Christ Jesus.
>
> —PHILIPPIANS 4:6–7

ARE YOU DEPRESSED?

Depression is a global problem. One in six people around the world will suffer from major depression at some point during their lives. It has been estimated that by the year 2020 depression will be the greatest disability worldwide.[3] So, how do you know if you're depressed?

A self-test

The following self-test has three questions. If you check more than two boxes per question, you may well be depressed. It isn't possible for this list to be all-inclusive, so if you aren't sure if you need help, I encourage you to consult your physician, pastoral counselor, or a mental health professional and take the positive steps they recommend along with the helping resources in this book. However, if you have any thoughts of harming yourself or others, that's a different situation. You should seek professional help immediately.

1. Much of the time, do you feel...

   ❑ Sad?
   ❑ Lethargic?
   ❑ Pessimistic?
   ❑ Hopeless?
   ❑ Worthless?
   ❑ Helpless?

2. Do you often...

   ❑ Have difficulty making decisions?
   ❑ Have trouble concentrating?
   ❑ Have memory problems?

3. Lately, have you...

   ❑ Lost interest in things that used to give you pleasure?
   ❑ Had problems at work or in school?
   ❑ Had problems with your family or friends?
   ❑ Isolated yourself from others? Or wanted to?
   ❑ Felt that you have no energy?
   ❑ Felt restless and irritable?

❑ Had trouble falling asleep, staying asleep, or getting up in the morning?

❑ Lost your appetite or gained weight?

❑ Experienced persistent headaches, stomachaches, backaches, and muscle or joint pains?

❑ Been drinking more alcoholic beverages than normal?

❑ Been taking more mood-altering medications than you used to?

❑ Engaged in risky behavior such as not wearing a seat belt or crossing streets without looking?

❑ Been thinking about death or your funeral?

❑ Been hurting yourself?[4]

And this same God who takes care of me will supply all your needs from his glorious riches, which have been given to us in Christ Jesus.

—PHILIPPIANS 4:19

THREE TYPES OF DEPRESSION

Depression is very misunderstood, perhaps because it can affect all three parts of your being—spirit, soul, and body. Any truly effective treatment for depression must address all three areas. Most of the time depression begins in your emotional and mental realm. Then it begins to affect your physical body, and finally it begins to affect your spiritual man. Usually, the problem actually begins in the mind because of a chemical imbalance. In any case, God has very real answers for this very real problem.

A **BIBLE CURE** *Health Fact*
Facts About Mood Disorders and Depression

- About 20.9 million adult Americans—9.5 percent of the population—suffer from a mood disorder, which is often accompanied by an anxiety disorder. Some people suffer from more than one disorder at the same time.[5]

- Major depressive disorder, which is more prevalent in women than men, affects approximately 14.8 million adults—that's about 6.7 percent of U.S. population.[6] This is the leading cause of disability in the United States for ages fifteen to forty-four.[7]

- Dysthymic disorder, which is mild depression, affects approximately 1.5 percent of the U.S. population,[8] or 3.3 million American adults.[9]

- Bipolar disorder affects approximately 5.7 million Americans, or about 2.6 percent of the U.S. adult population.[10]

The three major types of depression, also called depressive disorders or mood disorders, are:

Major depressive disorder—Major depression is an illness that can lead to an inability to function normally in society, and it can eventually lead to suicide. Major depression includes at least four of the symptoms in the Bible Cure Health Fact on the next page.

A **BIBLE CURE** Health Fact
The Symptoms of Major Depression

- Feelings of guilt, helplessness, hopelessness, or worthlessness
- Persistent sadness and a pessimistic attitude
- Difficulty concentrating
- Loss of interest or pleasure in normal activities that would bring pleasure, including sex
- Insomnia, early morning awakenings, or oversleeping
- Fatigue and lack of energy
- Weight loss or weight gain
- Slow movements and slow speech
- Suicidal thoughts*
- Agitation and irritability

---

* If you experience any thoughts of harming yourself or others, seek professional help immediately.

Dysthymic disorder—Dysthymia is characterized by a prevailing feeling of sadness. This disorder has symptoms similar to depression, but the symptoms are less intense and last at least two years. With this form of depression, a person is depressed most of the day and has two or more of the following symptoms:

- Poor appetite or overeating
- Insomnia or hypersomnia
- Low energy or fatigue
- Low self-esteem

- Poor concentration or difficulty making decisions
- Feelings of hopelessness

Bipolar disorder—This type of depression, also called manic-depressive disorder, is characterized by mood swings that range from extreme highs (mania) to extreme lows (depression). These mood swings can be very rapid and dramatic, but gradual shifts from mania to depression and back to mania again are more common. With this form of depression, a person may have periods where he is severely depressed, followed by periods of grandiose behavior where he is overconfident, overtalkative, and overactive, leading to embarrassing behavior and unwise decisions. In full mania, a person's judgment is seriously impaired. In depression, a person's symptoms are similar to those of major depression.

SEASONAL AFFECTIVE DISORDER (SAD)

Another type of depression worth mentioning is seasonal affective disorder, abbreviated as SAD. People suffering from SAD experience major mood changes when the seasons change, usually becoming depressed during the winter months but experiencing normal mental health the rest of the year. Light therapy has been found to be helpful in controlling depression associated with SAD. Exposure to high-intensity light from a light box for an hour a day for three to four weeks, or spending a week in a more sunny climate, will usually improve SAD.[11] You can also purchase light visors, which are simply visor caps with LED lights inside them, as they are a much more affordable option than a light box. (See Appendix B for more information.)

> And now, dear brothers and sisters...fix your thoughts on what is true, and honorable, and right, and pure, and lovely, and admirable. Think about things that are excellent and worthy of praise.
> —PHILIPPIANS 4:8

THEORIES ABOUT DEPRESSION

Why do people become depressed? Many theories about depression exist, such as the following:

- Depression is anger turned inward.

- Depression is caused by loss, such as the loss of a loved one or the loss of a job.

- The "learned helplessness theory" states that depression is caused by feelings of hopelessness and pessimism.[12]

- The "monoamine hypothesis" states that chemical imbalances cause depression, such as imbalances of monoamine chemicals, which include serotonin, epinephrine, and norepinephrine. These chemicals help the neurons in the nervous system transmit their electrical impulses properly. When an imbalance in these chemicals occur, mental health is affected adversely.[13]

I believe that there is some truth in all of the different theories on depression. However, I also believe that we need a solution that combines these theories in order to identify and eliminate the psychological factors as well as to correct imbalances in neurotransmitters in the brain. (A neurotransmitter is a substance that transmits nerve impulses across a synapse—the space between the junction of two nerve cells—much as a telephone wire transmits signals between two telephones. There are excitatory neurotransmitters, similar to an accelerator on a car, which increase the firing of neurons, and inhibitory neurotransmitters, which inhibit the firing of neurons, similar to a car's brakes. Neurotransmitters include serotonin, dopamine, GABA (gamma-aminobutyric acid), norepinephrine, and epinephrine. Each works in a different way, some inhibiting (GABA and serotonin), and others being excitatory (norepinephrine, epinephrine, and dopamine).

IS AGE A FACTOR?

Depression often begins in the early middle-age years (the average age of onset of the three mood disorders listed previously is between twenty-five and thirty-two).[14] But depression has increased dramatically in the last fifty years among children and adolescents. Children are becoming depressed at an earlier age. During adolescence, almost twice as many boys as girls are diagnosed. And over half of teens diagnosed with depression have a recurrence within seven years.[15]

In fact, since I first published this book in 1999, an alarming new trend has come to light. Research now shows that teens who engage in casual sex are three times more likely to be depressed than their friends who are still virgins; sexually active teen girls are three times as likely to attempt suicide and sexually active teen boys are *seven times* as likely to attempt suicide.[16]

A **BIBLE CURE** Health Tip

Recommended Reading for Parents

I encourage you to read a fascinating book called *Hooked*, written by Joe McIlhaney, MD, and Freda Bush, MD, for more information on the harmful, lifelong effects that casual sex has on children and teens. I think you will find it amazing to learn the chemical reactions in the body that are triggered by physical contact—even hugging—and affect our ability to properly trust and bond with others. When these triggers are activated outside of a stable, monogamous marital relationship, they can lead to damaged bonding mechanisms in the brain and a greater tendency toward depression, suicide, and more.

Long before scientists could identify what takes place chemically in the body, God warned us in His Word to abstain from sexual sin and avoid its consequences. Scriptures to read include: Romans 6:23, Ephesians 5:3–8, and Colossians 3:5–14.

Depression is also fairly common among the elderly. However, primary care doctors misdiagnose almost half of the cases of depression among the elderly. Often they are told that their loss of memory or sadness is a normal part of growing old, or that it is simply early senile dementia, which may develop into Alzheimer's disease.

Alzheimer's disease is characterized by loss of brain function, including impairment of memory, judgment, reasoning, speech, and socialization. Rarely striking before the age of fifty, the progression of this disease may take from a few months to as many as five years before complete loss of cognitive function.

Depression in the elderly is reversible. However, senile dementia is not. It is vitally important to make the correct diagnosis in order to give such individuals the appropriate care.

PHYSICAL FACTORS

Depression can also occur because of physical rather than psychological factors. Anyone experiencing depression should be tested to have organic factors ruled out. These include:

- Drug reactions
- Low thyroid function
- Anemia
- Nutritional deficiencies
- Alcohol abuse
- Illegal drug use
- Diabetes

- Chronic pain
- Cancer
- Heart disease
- Rheumatoid arthritis
- Sleep disturbances
- Low adrenal function

SEROTONIN: YOUR BODY'S "FEEL GOOD" CHEMICAL

Serotonin is a neurotransmitter, and neurotransmitters are chemicals in your brain cells that function as messengers between the nerve endings. Serotonin is absolutely critical for optimal brain functioning. Serotonin helps us to feel both calm and relaxed; it also helps us stay alert, energetic, happy, and well rested.

When serotonin levels are low (which can occur under chronic pain, long-term stress, insomnia, low-carbohydrate diets, excessive exercise, hormone imbalance), you will typically experience numerous symptoms, including problems sleeping, fatigue, craving for sugar and processed carbohydrates, loss of pleasure, irritability, and so forth. This will also cause your body not to function at its best.

> Those who love your instructions have great peace and do not stumble.
>
> —PSALM 119:165

Serotonin levels in our brains affect our mood, our sleep, whether we develop pain, migraine headaches, and even our appetites. Therefore, not having enough serotonin can lead to depression, anxiety, cravings for certain foods (especially sugars and starches), insomnia, and possibly even fibromyalgia and migraine headaches. It also can lead to chronic fatigue syndrome, premenstrual syndrome, and even bulimia.

By using brain-imaging techniques, for the first time researchers have seen inadequate serotonin in people who are experiencing depression. Researchers had suspected such a link between depression and serotonin activity for more than a quarter century, but there was no direct visual evidence until now.

In a study reported in the *American Journal of Psychiatry*, doctors from the New York State Psychiatric Institute, Columbia University, and the University of Pittsburgh compared six healthy people to six people with major depression who had not been medicated for at least two weeks. Using a serotonin-releasing drug, doctors observed significant increases, as well as decreases, in metabolic activity in the left and right regions of the brain in the healthy patients but not in the patients with depression.[17]

I will discuss nutritional supplements that I recommend to enable your body to make enough serotonin in chapter 4. But before I close this chapter, I want to explain to you the spiritual factors of depression.

SPIRITUAL FACTORS OF DEPRESSION

All types of depression have a common spiritual thread—the lack of God's joy in our lives. Without joy in our hearts, we run out of the energy needed to accomplish God's purpose for our lives. But when we are filled with the Holy Spirit, our thinking becomes more and more like God's thinking, and we are filled with the belief that anything is possible through faith.

> Don't let your hearts be troubled. Trust in God, and trust also in me.
>
> —JOHN 14:1

God promises to make our joy full. "I have told you these things so that you will be filled with my joy. Yes, your joy will overflow!" (John 15:11). I believe that the best antidepressant in your life is God's Word. Trust His promises and seek His overflowing joy through:

- Reading the Bible on a daily basis and meditating on His Word
- Being filled daily with God's Holy Spirit
- Memorizing scriptures
- Practicing thinking according to God's Word (Phil. 4:8), speaking faith-filled words, casting down thoughts that are contrary to God's Word, and practicing gratitude

Don't be discouraged. You are already making giant strides in being filled with His joy and freed from the spirit of depression and sadness.

A **BIBLE CURE** Prayer for You

Heavenly Father, I ask You to fill me with Your joy as I meditate on Your Word and Your great love for me. As I read this book, show me the things I need to apply to my life so that I can overcome depression and live the abundant, healthy life You desire for me. I also ask to be filled with Your Holy Spirit, so that I will think positive, creative thoughts that bring healing to my body, mind, and spirit. Amen.

A **BIBLE CURE** *Prescription*

Identifying Depression

List any symptoms of depression you may be suffering from.

_____

_____

_____

Now list any scriptures or positive affirmations you can think of to help you overcome depression in your life.

_____

_____

_____

_____

PEACE INSTEAD OF ANXIETY

D EPRESSION AND ANXIETY are often companions. If you are depressed, you may also experience symptoms associated with anxiety. Because of their prevalence, anxiety disorders have been called "the common cold of mental illness." Approximately 40 million American adults age eighteen and older—about 18.1 percent of people in the United States—have an anxiety disorder.[1] Here are a few more statistics you may not be aware of:

- About 80 percent of depressed individuals suffer psychological anxiety symptoms: unrealistic apprehension, fears, worry, agitation, irritability, or panic attacks.

- Some 60 percent of people with depression experience anxiety-related physical symptoms: headaches, irritable bowel syndrome, chronic fatigue, and chronic pain.

- Approximately 65 percent of depression sufferers experience sleep disturbances.

- About 20 percent feel agitated.

- Some 25 percent experience phobia.

- Approximately 17 percent report generalized anxiety symptoms.

- About 10 percent suffer panic attacks.[2]

Now I will explain the five categories of anxiety disorders.

GENERALIZED ANXIETY DISORDER

Approximately 6.8 million American adults—that's about 3.1 percent of people age eighteen and older—have generalized anxiety disorder, a condition associated with a constant state of worry and tension.[3] Your mind is preoccupied with worries and stresses, and your muscles are usually tensed up, especially muscles in the neck, shoulders, and back. You might be prone to clench your teeth, tighten your fists, tighten your buttocks, and fidget by shaking your legs. Similar to a car that is idling too high, your muscles are tense, ready to fight or flee, but you are stewing in your own stress juices.

> When you go through deep waters, I will be with you. When you go through rivers of difficulty, you will not drown. When you walk through the fire of oppression, you will not be burned up; the flames will not consume you.
>
> —ISAIAH 43:2

Anxiety is associated with many diseases, including tension headaches, migraine headaches, chronic neck pain, chronic back pain, TMJ, tendinitis (especially in the forearms), irritable bowel syndrome, palpitations, hives, chronic fatigue, and fibromyalgia, to mention only a few. If you are suffering from generalized anxiety disorder, it's likely that you have difficulty concentrating; tire easily; are restless, irritable, and fidgety; and have problems falling asleep and staying asleep.

PHOBIAS

A phobia is an extreme, exaggerated fear, and there are many different kinds of phobias. Allow me to briefly share some information about the phobias that occur most commonly in the United States.

- Approximately 15 million adults age eighteen and older—or about 6.8 percent of people—have *social phobia*.[4] Social phobia is a fear of social interaction or social performance, such as going to parties, meeting new people, and public speaking.

- Approximately 1.8 million American adults age eighteen and older, or 0.8 percent of the people, have *agoraphobia*.[5] Agoraphobia is a fear of being in public places, such as a shopping mall. These people typically worry about having a panic attack, having diarrhea, or vomiting in a public place. They usually fear leaving home, traveling, or being around a lot of people.

- Approximately 19.2 million American adults age eighteen and older—or about 8.7 percent of people—have some type of *specific phobia*.[6] Women are twice as likely as men to have them. Specific phobias are an extreme (and often unreasonable) fear of a specific object or situation. They avoid the feared object as much as possible.

As you can see from these statistics, specific phobias are the most common kind of phobia. They are also the most common form of anxiety disorder in America. According to the *Diagnostic and Statistical Manual of Mental Disorders*, fourth edition (DSM-IV), published by the American Psychiatric Association, specific phobias are grouped into five categories:

1. **Animal phobias** include fear of spiders, snakes, bugs, mice, dogs, for example. These are some of the most common specific phobias.

2. **Natural environment phobias** include fear of heights, storms, water, and so on.

3. **Blood-injection-injury phobias** include fear of being injured, seeing blood, receiving an injection, viewing or discussing medical procedures, and so forth.

4. **Situational phobias** include fear of driving over bridges or through tunnels, flying, riding in elevators, riding on public transportation, and other similar situations.

5. **Other phobias** include fear of choking, vomiting, falling down, loud sounds, balloons, clowns or other costumed characters, and so forth.[7]

OBSESSIVE-COMPULSIVE DISORDER

Approximately 2.2 million American adults age eighteen and older—that's about 1 percent of the population—have obsessive-compulsive disorder (OCD).[8] People suffering from OCD have compelling, disturbing thoughts that they are unable to get rid of. They use mental strategies or repetitive actions to decrease the anxiety brought on by these unhealthy thoughts. A common example is a person who is obsessive about germs and then compulsively washes his hands or cleans the house too frequently.

PANIC DISORDER

Approximately 6 million American adults age eighteen and older—or 2.7 percent of the population—suffer from panic disorder.[9] People with panic disorder have short bouts (usually lasting about ten minutes) of extremely intense fear or panic attacks in which they feel like they are going to die.

Other symptoms include pounding of the heart, hyperventilating, shortness of breath, chest pain, feeling like you are choking or smothering to death, trembling, light-headedness, tingling or numbness in the extremities, and feeling like you are "losing it" or going insane. I tell patients that it is similar to getting the accelerator of your car stuck to the floorboard while the car is in park.

A panic attack is a severe form of anxiety in which the heart races. Many times the person hyperventilates. He or she also has sweaty palms and extreme apprehension for no apparent reason. This is simply an adrenaline rush, which is a fight-or-flight reaction that simply occurs at the wrong time.

> Since God chose you to be the holy people he loves, you must clothe yourselves with tenderhearted mercy, kindness, humility, gentleness, and patience. Make allowance for each other's faults, and forgive anyone who offends you. Remember, the Lord forgave you, so you must forgive others. Above all, clothe yourselves with love, which binds us all together in perfect harmony. And let the peace that comes from Christ rule in your hearts. For as members of one body you are called to live in peace. And always be thankful.
> —COLOSSIANS 3:12–15

One of the best ways to prevent a panic attack is to breathe deeply. Inhale slowly through your nose while counting to four. Hold your breath for approximately four seconds; then exhale slowly over a four-second period through your mouth. Continue to do this until the panic attack subsides.

You will learn about certain amino acids that are very beneficial for anxiety states. The fight-or-flight response involved with panic attacks commonly drains the adrenal glands. These important glands need to be supported by nutritional supplements. Certain herbs are also helpful for reducing anxiety. See chapter 5 for a complete protocol of natural supplements I recommend for anxiety.

POST-TRAUMATIC STRESS DISORDER

Approximately 7.7 million adults age eighteen and older—or about 3.5 percent of the population—have post-traumatic stress disorder (PTSD).[10] Typically, someone with PTSD has been the victim of a major trauma, such as a rape, sexual abuse, armed robbery, or a very humiliating experience. PTSD is also associated with war trauma, torture, a traumatic accident or an injury, or surviving a natural disaster such as an earthquake or a hurricane.

PTSD may occur shortly after the trauma or years later. People suffering from PTSD usually relive their trauma in their minds, and it causes crippling anxiety. I find that thought field therapy is very useful for this form of anxiety, as well as phobias and other forms of anxiety.

DEFEATING ANXIETY DISORDERS

I commonly treat patients with phobias, PTSD, and OCD with thought field therapy as well as forgiveness therapy. Psychologist Roger Callahan developed thought field therapy, and he states that

70 to 80 percent of individuals can expect to have their negative emotions completely resolved.[11] (See Appendix B for information about this therapy.)

Forgiveness therapy is something I have developed in my own practice over the past twenty years, and many of my patients have seen amazing results after this therapy.

Both of these therapies require professional assistance, but throughout this book I will be leading you through steps you can take on your own to defeat anxiety and enter into God's perfect peace.

But those who trust in the LORD will find new strength. They will soar high on wings like eagles. They will run and not grow weary. They will walk and not faint.

—ISAIAH 40:31

THE PRESCRIPTION OF GOD'S WORD

The Word of God is an effective antidote in daily life for both depression and anxiety. God has created natural ways as well as a spiritual prescription for battling and defeating depression and anxiety in your life. In this chapter, you have discovered several positive steps to overcome anxiety. Don't turn back or become discouraged. Continue to move forward with God as you live in His joy and peace.

Pray often, quote scriptures in your prayers, and meditate on the promises of God. Daily read the Word of God, and confess aloud scriptures that come against fear and worry. You should practice casting down thoughts that are contrary to God's Word. You can also purchase a relaxation CD at a bookstore.

Practice gratitude, and help people less fortunate than you. Years ago I read a story about a man who complained because he had no shoes until he met a man who had no feet.

I recommend that all my patients with anxiety quote specific scriptures aloud three times a day before meals, meditate on them throughout the day, and again quote the scriptures before going to bed.

In Appendix A of this book are wonderful scriptures for overcoming anxiety. Write them down, memorize them, and meditate on them. Put them in places where you can see them—attach sticky notes to your computer or anchor scriptures with magnets on your refrigerator.

The Word of God is an effective antidote in daily life for both depression and anxiety. God has created natural ways as well as a spiritual prescription for battling and defeating depression and anxiety in your life.

A **BIBLE CURE** Prayer for You

Heavenly Father, I realize that fear does not come from You. I ask You to break the strongholds of fear, worry, and anxiety in my life. I receive the power, love, and sound mind you have promised to me in Your Word. I put my trust in You and rest in Your perfect peace, a peace that passes all human understanding. Amen.

A **BIBLE CURE** Prescription

Overcoming Anxiety

List any symptoms of anxiety you have identified after reading this chapter.

_____

_____

_____

Now describe steps you can begin to take to overcome anxiety.

_____

_____

_____

_____

_____

_____

Review what you have listed. Have you included:

- ❑ Forgiving others
- ❑ Prayer
- ❑ Meditating on God's Word
- ❑ Confessing scriptures
- ❑ Casting down thoughts contrary to God's Word
- ❑ Daily reading the Bible
- ❑ Memorizing scriptures
- ❑ Being filled daily with God's Holy Spirit
- ❑ Practicing gratitude

3

JOY-FILLED LIVING WITH NEW THOUGHT PATTERNS

ONE DAY A minister went to preach at another pastor's church and stayed in the pastor's guest bedroom. When he arrived at the pastor's home, he was very tired and simply ate dinner with the pastor and his wife and then promptly went to bed.

In the middle of the night he was suddenly awakened by a rustling noise coming from the corner of the bedroom. He quickly sat up in bed, but he was unable to see clearly since the room was very dark. But as his eyes adjusted to the light, he was able to see a large dark image in the corner of the room that appeared to be moving and making a strange rustling type of noise.

He was very afraid, thinking that a ghost, apparition, or dark ominous spiritual presence had entered the room. He immediately began to pray, and after a few minutes he was relieved to see that the apparition had stopped moving and the strange noise had ceased.

However, the strange apparition would begin to move again and make the strange noise every twenty minutes or so. This continued to occur throughout the entire night, and he remained staring at the corner of the room. He was very anxious, fearful, and trembling as he continued to watch and pray throughout the night.

Finally, in the morning when the first rays of dawn appeared, the minister was then able to see clearly. What he had been seeing was not an apparition at all. What he was seeing was actually an old dark raincoat hanging on a coat rack in the corner of the bedroom! It would rustle and move as the air conditioning vent blew on it.

The minister couldn't believe he had wasted so much time and energy and lost a good night's sleep worrying about something he had actually concocted in his mind. It wasn't even real!

This is similar to the distortional thought patterns that we create in our minds. Most of these thought patterns are imaginary and not based on facts. This book will act as a light similar to the first rays of dawn, enabling to you to recognize these patterns and mind-sets. In this chapter I will teach you how to tear down strongholds and mind-sets and replace them with the Word of God. When these strongholds and mind-sets are torn down, you will learn how to practice gratitude and then enter into the peace of God.

It All Starts With Your Thoughts

Your interpretation of traumatic events and your mental programming form thoughts that become beliefs. Your beliefs then lead to feelings that lead to choices, words, actions or behaviors, and reactions. When you continue to repeat behaviors, words, choices, and reactions, these will eventually lead to habits. Habits then form your character. Your character then determines your destiny. I like the way Dr. David Yonggi Cho explains the effects of our thoughts on our actions in his book *Fourth Dimensional Living in a Three Dimensional World*:

> To the extent that we mentally map out our plans for success and carry out those plans accordingly, our assurance of success increases. However, if a person is more focused on failure than on success, the likelihood of his or her failure will increase. When our minds dwell upon success, our thinking will yield positive outcomes, and

> the fulfillment of our dreams will be expedited....Once
> you start believing that something is possible, the likeli-
> hood of your taking the action to achieve that goal will
> greatly increase....Thinking influences your feelings and
> behaviors, as well as your physical body....That is why
> we must begin thinking in God's ways, not our own.[1]

Your thoughts affect not only your physical life but your spiritual life as well. Dr. Cho says that your thinking is like "spiritual
breathing."[2] He means that your thinking is as vital to your spiritual life as breathing is to your physical life. Because it affects
everything you do, your thinking is the way God carries out His
plans in your life. I encourage you to read Dr. Cho's book *Fourth
Dimensional Living in a Three Dimensional World* for more information on the power our thoughts have in our lives.

Both depression and anxiety are thought disorders. When you
learn to tune in to your feelings and begin to capture anxiety-
provoking thoughts and beliefs, you can then replace these
automatic thoughts and beliefs with God's Word, which will
resolve both depression and anxiety. You can literally change your
thinking and change your life.

It is impossible to dissect every thought because you have literally tens of thousands of thoughts every day. However, you can
tune in to your feelings. Feelings can then alert you to what you
are thinking, which is usually at the root of your anxiety.

In 2 Corinthians 10:4–5, Paul states, "For the weapons of our
warfare are not carnal, but mighty through God to the pulling down
of strong holds, casting down imaginations and every high thing
that exalteth itself against the knowledge of God, and bringing into
captivity every thought to the obedience of Christ" (KJV).

Realize that these two verses in 2 Corinthians talk about
thoughts, imaginations, and strongholds. An anxious thought will

become an anxious imagination or belief, which, if dwelt upon, over time will become a stronghold or a mind-set.

To help you understand this process, think of the preset radio stations on a radio dial. When you push one button, you're listening to the talk radio station, and when you push another button, the Christian music station is tuned in.

Your preset belief system, usually formed in childhood, eventually becomes a mind-set or what is called a stronghold in the passage from 2 Corinthians. When you operate from preset beliefs, you feel anxious without even knowing why. You then act on these beliefs so much that you bypass even thinking about them and simply feel anxious. In other words, you react before you think.

You will learn, when anxious feelings occur, to track your anxiety triggers, thoughts, and beliefs. Then as you reprogram these thoughts and beliefs, anxiety will subside and eventually go.

Romans 8:5–6 says, "For those who live according to the flesh set their minds on the things of the flesh, but those who live according to the Spirit, the things of the Spirit. For to be carnally minded is death, but to be spiritually minded is life and peace" (NKJV).

This verse shows us the importance of dwelling on spiritual thinking rather than worldly ("of the flesh") thinking. The things we dwell on create mind-sets. Worldly mind-sets lead to depression and anxiety, but spiritual mind-sets lead to life and peace. Peace is the opposite of anxiety, and we can develop peace by reprogramming and tearing down all mind-sets or strongholds contrary to God's Word and replacing them with scriptures.

DETECTING VIRUSES IN YOUR MENTAL COMPUTER

Most of the thought patterns you have today have been learned from your parents or other figures of authority. When you were born, your mind was like a brand-new computer with brand-new software. Your thinking "powers up" your computer and launches the "operating software" that runs your life. Your parents or the people who raised you were the primary programmers of that operating software. If your parents programmed it with praise, contentment, gratitude, love, and joy, you are likely to go through life with these types of attitudes and expectations.

> Since you have heard about Jesus and have learned the truth that comes from him, throw off your old sinful nature and your former way of life, which is corrupted by lust and deception. Instead, let the Spirit renew your thoughts and attitudes. Put on your new nature, created to be like God—truly righteous and holy.
> —EPHESIANS 4:21–24

But if they programmed it with worry, you will be prone to worry; if they programmed it with fear, your automatic reaction is fear; if they programmed it with expecting the worst, you will expect the worst. Your parents may have programmed limitation into your thought patterns by telling you that you will never be smart enough, you will never make it, you will never be successful, or you are not talented enough.

My purpose is not to have you start blaming your parents—after all, their thought patterns were likely programmed by their parents, who were programmed by their parents, and so on. My goal is simply to help you understand where your thought patterns originated.

It actually all began when Adam and Even disobeyed God in the Garden of Eden. They allowed the virus of sin to infect the hardware of humanity, and from that point on, every heart and mind has been infected. We have been programmed with depraved thinking, negativity, hopelessness, anger, and insecurity.

When Christians are born again, we receive Christ's forgiveness for our sins and invite Him into our *hearts*, but many Christians never purge the bad software from their *minds* even though the virus of sin has been removed. We need to learn to identify the feelings, thoughts, and beliefs that are distortional and replace them with the Word of God until God's thoughts and beliefs are automatic in our minds and in our hearts.

Think about our computer virus illustration for a moment. What happens when a virus gets into even the best computer and contaminates its software? At first, certain parts of the computer will not function properly, and it loses speed. Eventually the computer freezes and eventually may not run anymore.

So it is with your mind. Sinful viruses infect your life, contaminating your software with bitterness, unforgiveness, resentment, hatred, jealousy, anger, rage, and more. If allowed to spread throughout your system, they can affect your ability to function properly, just like a computer. Soon, not only are your mental health and emotional health affected, but your physical health suffers too, leading to depression, anxiety, and a host of physical diseases.

I wholeheartedly believe that these negative thought processes and toxic emotions are at the root of many diseases and health problems. In my practice, I lead many patients through something I call "forgiveness therapy" as an initial step in their treatment.

I then teach them how to recognize feelings, beliefs, and thoughts that trigger depression and anxiety. These patients learn to replace their distortional thought patterns and beliefs with God's Word. I also emphasize the importance of practicing contentment, gratitude, and joy to literally insulate the heart and mind from anxiety and depression. (I will expand on this later in this book.)

However, too many doctors, psychologists, and psychiatrists are treating depression and anxiety with medication or psychotherapy that simply treats the symptoms; they never get to the root cause.

COGNITIVE-BEHAVIORAL THERAPY

Dr. Aaron Beck was a psychiatrist trained in the standard psychiatry of his day. Decades ago, he used analysis of his patients' dreams in order to find clues to their depression, anxiety, and anger. He also used free association, which was a standard Freudian tool to have a patient discuss their thoughts as they occur.

By the 1960s, Dr. Beck was dissatisfied with this approach. He found that when his patients let their thoughts run free, they typically left their sessions feeling worse instead of better, but when he helped patients develop a practical approach to problem solving, they tended to improve significantly faster.

Based on these findings, Dr. Beck began to work with his patients to help them recognize, dispute, and reprogram their automatic thought patterns. This later became known as cognitive therapy or cognitive-behavioral therapy.

In cognitive-behavioral therapy, a patient learns to examine his thinking and question any negative beliefs, assumptions, or feelings. When negative thought patterns—"If something bad is going to happen, it will happen to me"—are broken, the painful expectations that accompany them lose their self-fulfilling power, and most people experience a dramatic improvement.

What I have learned over the years in referring patients to a cognitive-behavioral therapist is that many improve, but most still need to be programmed with the Word of God (the Bible).

In Matthew 13, in the parable of the wheat and the tares, the parable states that the kingdom of heaven is like a farmer planting seeds in his field, but at night after the workers left, his enemy came and planted weeds among the wheat.

Distortional thoughts are like weeds planted in your mind and heart. They grow up to become huge strongholds that can have you literally imprisoned in depression and anxiety.

To defeat these strongholds, you have to learn to recognize and pull up these weeds and then plant the "incorruptible seed" of God's Word, which prevents more weeds from growing. When this seed of the Word of God is planted in your mind and heart, it literally produces a harvest of peace, joy, gratitude, and all of the remaining fruit of the Spirit. (See Galatians 5:22–23.)

You should not be content to merely read God's Word; you need to have it "planted" in your heart. This means you need to have certain Scripture verses committed to memory so you can recall them anytime you need to spiritually combat any negative, distortional thoughts.

The good news is that there are only ten major distortional beliefs that need to be reprogrammed. I've listed some of these in my books *Stress Less* and *Deadly Emotions*. The distortional thought patterns listed below are the ten most common patterns I encounter in my patients. They are similar to ten distortional thought processes identified by Dr. David Burns, a renowned psychiatrist and author of *Feeling Good*. Some of these distortional beliefs are associated with depression, some with anxiety, and some with both.

Following each distortional thought pattern below, I've added a confession based on God's Word that you can say to yourself each time you are being caught up in one of these negative thought patterns.

DISTORTIONAL THOUGHT PATTERNS

1. "What if" thinking
This distortional thinking is very common with anxious individuals. Examples include: "What if I lose my job?" "What if I lose

my home?" "What if my children get hooked on drugs?" "What if I have a heart attack?" "What if I get cancer?"

Realize that "what if" thinking breeds anxiety and fear. If you focus on "what if," your fear *grows*; however, if you focus on God's Word, your fear *goes*. Eliminate this "what if" thinking. It shatters faith, and without faith, it is impossible to please God.

Learn to replace "what if" with what God's Word says: God always causes me to triumph. I can do all things through Christ who strengthens me. If God be for me, who can be against me? God makes all things to work together for good to those who love Him. God *is* working on your behalf. These are promises in His Word, and you know you can count on them.

Every time you speak what God's Word says, it is similar to planting a seed in a garden. Every time you confess God's Word, it's similar to watering your planted seed. But every time you say, "What if," it is similar to digging up the seed you planted. So stop saying, "What if?"

Confession from God's Word

I confess that all things are possible to those who believe (Mark 9:23). I lay on the altar the words "what if." I realize that "what if" thing and "what if" words destroy faith, and without faith it is impossible to please God. I refuse to dig up the precious seeds of God's promises by speaking "what if." Instead, I will speak God's promises and ask myself, "What does God's Word say?"

2. Catastrophizing

I call this kind of thinking "awfulizing" because the mind actually magnifies unpleasant events and transforms them into something more awful, terrible, or horrible than they really are. In this mind-set, a person makes a mountain out of a molehill. I often describe catastrophizing people as spending ten dollars' worth of energy on a two-cent problem.

Catastrophizing words include *awful, terrible, horrible, unbearable, dreadful, devastating, intolerable,* and *hopeless.* These are extreme words that can transform a minor circumstance into a major stressor and create a lot of anxiety. Similar to pouring lighter fluid on a burning fire, these inflammatory words fuel anxiety.

The only way to put out the fire is to learn to eliminate these inflammatory words from your vocabulary and replace them with more practical, realistic, and less emotionally charged words, such as *unfortunate, inconvenient, difficult, bothersome, inappropriate, uncomfortable,* or *disagreeable.*

Stop the drama! Learn to identify and eliminate catastrophizing thinking. Ask your spouse or a close friend to help you identify catastrophizing words, and learn to replace these thoughts with affirmations like the following confession.

Confession from God's Word

Instead of awfulizing, I choose faith-building words, because "we know that God causes everything to work together for the good of those who love God" (Rom. 8:28). I replace awfulizing words with less emotionally charged words, such as *unfortunate* or *inconvenient.* I will continue to practice this pattern of thinking until it becomes automatic, making it a habit and mind-set.

3. Habitually expecting the worst outcome

This is a common distortional thought process in both anxious and depressed individuals. They are programmed with "Murphy's Law mentality." Remember Murphy's Law? It states that if anything *can* go wrong, it probably *will.*

Examples of this form of thinking include: "If something bad is going to happen, it will probably happen to me." "My boss did not even acknowledge me today, so I am sure she hates me and will probably fire me." "My husband is late for dinner, so I am sure he is having an affair." "My child has a fever and headache; I am sure he has spinal meningitis."

Realize that when you repeatedly think about something, you create the potential for these thoughts to become self-fulfilling prophecies. By imagining the worst, you are actually unknowingly attracting bad circumstances to your life like a magnet. Galatians 6:7 says, "Do not be deceived, God is not mocked; for whatever a man sows, that he will also reap" (NKJV). In other words, if you continue to plant worst-case-scenario thoughts, you will eventually reap a worst-case-scenario harvest.

Instead of expecting the worst possible outcome, begin to expect something good to happen to you.

Confession from God's Word

As it says in Psalm 91:10, no evil will befall my family or me, nor will any plague come near my dwelling. I cast down the thought pattern of expecting the worst, and I wholly confess that something good is going to happen to my family and me today and every day. I realize that all things work together for good to those who love God. My loved ones and I are under God's protection.

4. Leaping to conclusions

I call these people who leap to conclusions the "grim leapers," because this distortional thought pattern commonly leads to depression and anxiety. They mistakenly believe that they know what another person is thinking without having any facts to support it. They repeatedly and habitually make negative assumptions that fuel depression and anxiety.

For example, you walk into your favorite restaurant and see two of your friends having lunch together without you. They look at you and then whisper something to one another. You immediately assume that they have decided to leave you out of the friendship and they are picking you apart or pointing out some physical flaw. In reality, they are whispering that they are planning a surprise birthday party for you at the restaurant and hope you don't figure it out now that you've spotted them.

Begin to identify when you are jumping to conclusions. Challenge yourself to expect the best of the other person. Instead of becoming anxious about things you don't even know are real, determine to wait until you have more information before drawing a conclusion about the situation.

Confession from God's Word

I refuse to leap to conclusions, but instead I will practice 1 Corinthians 13:7, which says that love "is ever ready to believe the best of every person" (AMP). I refuse to leap to conclusions, but instead I will capture these thoughts and bring them into line with God's Word. Instead of leaping, I choose to guard my heart and practice loving everyone I come in contact with.

5. Black-and-white thinking

If you suffer from this thought pattern, you view circumstances and events in black and white with no shades of gray. You are probably a perfectionist who sees your work as either flawless or worthless. You may perceive an average job performance evaluation or an average grade as a complete failure. In your mind-set, there is no second place. First place is the only winning spot; everyone else is a loser.

This distortional thought pattern sets you up for failure, disappointment, depression, and anxiety. You are always just one mistake away from total failure. You will work endless hours to make the assignment perfect, or you may procrastinate and never finish the assignment because if it is not perfect, you feel it is worthless.

Also, if you struggle with perfectionism, you will need to watch that you don't fall into the trap of comparisons. Making comparisons is the opposite of contentment. Paul said in Philippians 4:11, "I have learned how to be content with whatever I have." Understand that when you compare, you will usually despair.

Quit focusing on what you do not have and start thanking God for what you do have. Instead of complaining about your old car, start thanking God for even having a car. The majority of people in the world do not even own a car. The Word of God admonishes us about complaining. In Philippians 2:14 the Bible says, "Do all things without grumbling and faultfinding and complaining" (AMP).

Confession from God's Word

I realize that only Jesus was perfect and that I can never be perfect. I choose to do my best and not compare myself to others. I always forgive myself, accept myself, and love myself unconditionally, even if I make a mistake. (Now say this to yourself as you look in the mirror every morning: "I forgive myself, accept myself, and love myself unconditionally, even if I make a mistake.")

6. Unenforceable rules

This person is usually trapped in anxiety. He typically has a rigid set of rules about what *should*, *must*, or *ought to* be done, and he tries to put people and events into his little box. His expectations are unrealistic because he has no control over circumstances or other people.

The more unrealistic and unenforceable the rules are, the greater his disappointment. That disappointment usually plays out as worry, frustration, irritation, guilt, depression, or anxiety.

An example of this type of thinking includes: "They should stop driving so recklessly and should stop cutting me off in traffic."

If you struggle with this thought pattern, you expect that people should do certain things, society should act a particular way, or situations should always turn out in an expected fashion. However, life is not fair, and people and situations will eventually let you down. This mind-set will keep you uptight, frustrated, angry, bitter, and eventually will lead to depression and/or anxiety.

The healthy thinker knows that the only *should* statement a person needs to make is: "I should practice mercy, which is forgiveness." People and situations usually don't turn out the way we want them to turn out. Jesus said in Matthew 5:7, "God blesses those who are merciful, for they will be shown mercy." In other words, when I practice giving mercy instead of unenforceable rules, I will receive mercy.

It reminds me of the musical *Les Misérables*. Jean Valjean was put in prison for stealing a loaf of bread and served many years. He eventually got out of prison and stole some expensive candlesticks and other expensive items from a priest's home. When he was arrested and taken to the priest's home, even though Jean had stolen the priest's items, the priest forgave him and told the authorities he had given the items to Jean. The gift of mercy was so great that Jean devoted the rest of his life to doing good.

Confession from God's Word

I release all unenforceable rules; instead I will love and show mercy to everyone I come in contact with and overlook how I think they should act or behave. Love keeps no record of wrong, so I throw out my record-keeping book.

I eliminate *should* statements from my vocabulary and replace them with "I prefer" and "I would like to." I cast down *should* statements and bring them into captivity to the obedience of Christ.

7. Labeling

The old adage of "Sticks and stones may break my bones, but words will never hurt me" is absolutely false. Words can hurt emotionally and create a belief system that leads to depression and anxiety.

Just as we pull weeds in a garden, we need to pull these words out and eliminate them from our vocabulary. Examples of common labels we use for ourselves or others include idiot, jerk, loser, klutz, failure, nerd, stupid, pitiful, pathetic, moron, and so on. I commonly hear children and parents joking around in my office, calling each other one or more of these names.

I would like to remind people that these degrading words do have the potential to fuel distortional thought patterns that lead to failure, loser mentality, depression, and anxiety. These labels destroy self-esteem and self-worth, and as a result, many never accept, love, or forgive themselves.

Confession from God's Word

I am a new creature in Christ Jesus according to 2 Corinthians 5:17, and I cancel out every negative, demeaning, and derogatory label spoken over me. I repent for labeling other people. I refuse to label anyone with a negative label. I choose to see myself and others the way God sees us. God has called me "precious," "beloved," and the apple of His eye, and I am His child.

8. Negative filter

This person typically discounts all information that is positive or good. He usually discounts anything positive. In other words, he may hear a compliment but usually discounts it or discredits it.

Instead he hears and remembers mainly criticisms and negative information. He focuses completely on the bad and retains it while allowing anything good to slip away. He often focuses on his or others' weaknesses and forgets about strengths, making him likely to be very critical of himself and other people.

No one in this world is perfect; neither is anyone competent at everything. But people who dwell on their incompetencies, shortcomings, or mistakes may fall into a pit of hopelessness. That's why I call this thought pattern "pit thinking." It is commonly associated with depression. If you are a "pit thinker," you probably overgeneralize, taking one unpleasant circumstance and believing that it represents a trend of how your life will proceed. You probably use the words *always* and *never*. You think, "I will always be like this." "I will never change." Realize that words such as *always* and *never* are absolute words, setting you up for the belief that you cannot change.

If this sounds like something you struggle with, I challenge you to enjoy the next compliment you receive. There is nothing prideful about graciously accepting praise or a compliment when rightfully given. Not only will this reduce anxiety, but it will also add richness to your life. Years ago I heard a pastor say, "Remember your victories and successes, but forget your failures and shortcomings."

Confession from God's Word

I repent of this negative thought pattern. I now boldly confess Isaiah 61:3. He gives me the garment of praise for the spirit of heaviness. I take off the old garment of a negative mental filter, and I put on the new garment of praise and thanksgiving.

I choose only positive thoughts according to Philippines 4:8, which says to think about things that are true, honest, just, pure, lovely, of good report, virtuous, and praiseworthy. God has changed my filter to a positive filter. He brought me out of a horrible pit and has put a new song in my mouth of praise and thanksgiving to God. While the late night news is true, honest, and just, rarely is it pure, lovely, a good report, virtuous, or praiseworthy. I will filter all thoughts, media, TV shows, movies, and even my words through all the criteria of Philippians 4:8. If anything falls short of every criterion, I refuse to watch it, think it, or speak it out of my mouth.

9. Emotional reasoning

A person with this distortional thought pattern treats her feelings as facts. If she *feels* depressed or anxious, she believes that something bad is going to happen to her. If she *feels* incompetent, then she thinks she must be doing a lousy job. If she *feels* rejected by others, then she believes she must be worthless. If she *feels* hopeless about taking an exam, she might not even show up to take it. She struggles with the temptation to give up because her emotions make her feel defeated.

The healthy thinker separates her emotions from her overall self-worth. She can separate current feelings from future events. She realizes that in spite of how she is feeling, she can change the outcome of her situation by confessing, believing, and meditating on God's promises, and expecting His will to come to pass in any situation.

Realize that negative feelings are a sign that you are thinking negative, depressing thoughts. You need to immediately tune in to the thoughts or beliefs that are at the root of the emotion and simply change the channel of your mind to the gratitude channel.

Confession from God's Word

I will not be influenced by my emotions or feelings, because the just shall live by faith (Heb. 10:38) and it is impossible to please God without faith (Heb. 11:6). I will be steadfast because the truth of my situation is based on what God *says*, not on what I *feel*. In Galatians 6:9 Paul said, "And let us not be weary in well doing: for in due season we shall reap, if we faint not" (KJV). I will hold fast to the confession of my hope without wavering, for He who promised is faithful. I believe the promises God has made concerning me, and I refuse to allow my emotions to control me.

10. The blame game

Many depressed and anxious people are stuck in a trap of blaming others or God. This creates a vicious circle of thinking and feeling that leads to anger, resentment, bitterness, depression, and anxiety.

People with a victim mentality fit within this group of faulty thinkers. They feel that they are victims of circumstances and everything bad that happens to them is someone else's fault. An example of this form of thinking includes: "It's her fault [pointing to his wife] that I lost my job because she made me late by not having my breakfast ready." This person has not taken responsibility.

To break free from this distortional thought pattern, it's important to realize that the blame game keeps you from taking responsibility for your own failures and shifts the blame onto someone else. Blame locks you in the past; it also prevents you from examining yourself and recognizing and removing thought patterns and mind-sets that continue to sabotage your life. Instead of blaming, take responsibility for your mistakes, forgive yourself, and refuse to blame someone else. If it is someone else's fault, then simply forgive them. Realize that forgiveness is a decision, not a feeling. Choose today to forgive rather than blame—not for the sake of the other person, but for the sake of your own emotional and physical well-being.

Confession from God's Word

I release all blame toward myself, toward others, and toward God. God's Word says, "Blessed are the merciful, for they shall obtain mercy." I choose to forgive and cancel the debt even though I was hurt. Forgiveness is a commandment, and I realize if I do not forgive, I will not be forgiven (Mark 11:25–26). I refuse to blame or rehash any hurt or pain. I realize that forgiveness is a decision and not a feeling. I choose to forgive instead of blame.

PUTTING YOUR THOUGHT PATTERNS ON TRIAL

Now that we have identified the ten major distortional thought patterns related to depression and anxiety, we need to learn to recognize these patterns.

Most of these thoughts are under the radar because you have been practicing them so much that they have become mind-sets. You may fly off the handle or become anxious over a minor event or circumstance without even thinking about it, or you feel stress, depression, or anxiety, and you don't even realize that you don't have to react this way.

In order to recognize these patterns, you must first tune in to your feelings and take inventory of what you are thinking. By monitoring your feelings you will eventually be able to figure out which thoughts and beliefs triggered your anxiety. I call these "thought triggers." The thought triggers are almost always one of these ten distortional thought patterns that have become ingrained in your thinking similar to a computer virus. The first step in breaking this stronghold is to identify these triggers.

It is also helpful to journal your thoughts, to write down exactly what is going through your mind when you are feeling depressed or anxious. (Remember, depressed or anxious feelings mean that you are usually thinking a distortional thought pattern or reliving or rehashing a traumatic event.)

Next, compare the thoughts you've written down in your journal to the list of ten distortional thought patterns. Then begin confessing the positive confessions from God's Word that correspond to the negative thoughts you've identified in your journal.

I call this "taking your distortional thought patterns to court." You see, most people believe that these patterns are true since they have been thinking this way all of their lives. However, you need to put these thought patterns and assumptions on trial, convict them, imprison them, and then reprogram them with God's Word. Unfortunately, most Christians have not done this, and that is why just as many Christians have depression and anxiety as non-Christians.

I also recommend that you seek the advice of a good cognitive-behavioral therapist (CBT) to ensure that you identify and change these distortional thought patterns. (Please refer to Appendix B for information.) I commonly refer my patients to a CBT and find that people with depression as well as all types of anxiety disorders will usually benefit significantly from cognitive-behavioral therapy.

A **BIBLE CURE** Prayer for You

Heavenly Father, I begin today to reprogram the negative thoughts that have me trapped in a cycle of depression, anxiety, and worry. I choose to replace them with positive thoughts based on Your Word. Help me to recognize distortional thinking when it happens and to replace it with the reality of how You see me and my situation. Amen.

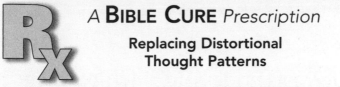

A **BIBLE CURE** *Prescription*

Replacing Distortional Thought Patterns

List any common situations that cause you to become depressed or anxious.

_____

_____

_____

List any distortional thoughts or beliefs that may be the underlying cause of these stressful situations.

_____

_____

_____

Now list the scriptures or positive affirmations you can use to replace these distortional thoughts.

_____

_____

_____

_____

_____

_____

4

JOY-FILLED LIVING WITH PROPER NUTRITION AND DIET

T HE THINGS YOU eat and the things you do can contribute to feelings of depression. Some of our most harmful lifestyle and nutritional choices include drinking alcohol; smoking cigarettes; eating too much sugar; drinking too much caffeine; eating a diet rich in processed foods such as white bread, white flour, white rice, and pasta; eating fast food and junk food; and being addicted to prescription and street drugs.

You can make right nutritional choices today to replace depression with joy. You may think, "I feel too depressed to make right choices." If that's your thought, then replace it immediately with this: "For I can do everything through Christ, who gives me strength" (Phil. 4:13).

The delicate balance of chemicals in your brain is strongly affected when you eat too few complex carbohydrates (such as eating a low-carb diet), have low blood sugar or high blood sugar (which is prediabetes or diabetes), drink too much caffeine, have too much stress or too little sleep, or have critical nutritional deficiencies. All these factors lower your levels of *serotonin,* which we discussed in chapter 1. This is why proper lifestyle and dietary choices are critical if you want to prevent depression.

THE CONNECTION BETWEEN FOOD AND MOOD

The brain depends on a steady supply of sugar from the blood, and the ideal amount that the brain desires falls within a narrow range. When we eat too many foods high in sugar or too many processed carbohydrates, the blood sugar rises too high, which causes insulin levels to rise in order to lower the blood sugar. As a result of high sugar followed by high insulin levels, many people develop cloudy thinking and become drowsy and desire to take a nap.

However, on the opposite end of the spectrum, when your blood sugar falls too low, you typically become hungry. If you do not eat within a certain period of time, the blood sugar can actually drop even lower. When your brain does not receive adequate blood sugar, you, as well as most individuals, may become irritable, impatient, angry, weak, shaky, fatigued, depressed, or anxious.

So, what do most people do when their blood sugar is low and they're experiencing these symptoms? They reach for a Starbucks coffee, a doughnut, a soda, or a candy bar! These do quickly raise your blood sugar, but this is only a quick fix and actually makes your blood sugar drop again a few hours later.

So many Americans are caught in these blood sugar swings and do not realize that a balanced diet containing plenty of fiber, the proper ratio of good protein with healthy fats with high-fiber complex carbohydrates, and at least three meals a day—a healthy breakfast, healthy lunch, and healthy dinner—as well as two to three healthy, balanced snacks (again with adequate fiber), prevents these blood sugar swings. Unfortunately, many people who experience depression and anxiety are caught in this "roller-coaster" blood sugar cycle. It is simply due to wrong food choices.

Many individuals with depression and anxiety have candida

overgrowth in the intestinal tract from taking antibiotics, cortisone medications, hormones; from excessive stress or consuming excessive amounts of sugar or processed starches such as white flour; or from diabetes or prediabetes. Over the years I have seen a definite association with many patients with depression and anxiety also having candida and craving sugar and products made from white flour. For more information on this topic, refer to *The Bible Cure for Candida and Yeast Infections.*

Also, I've found that certain foods might be well tolerated by most people but can actually worsen the symptoms of depression and anxiety in other people. Some psychiatrists have written about this and described the way that some of their patients were greatly impacted by their choices of certain foods. Some patients experienced symptoms such as sadness and crying; others had increased anxiety and panic.

A BIBLE CURE *Health Fact*

Opiates in Milk and Wheat?

According to Dr. Charles Parker, "The peptides from gluten and casein are important because they react with opiate receptors in the brain, thus mimicking the effects of opiate drugs like heroin and morphine."[1] This means that the gluten in wheat and the casein in milk have the potential to cause addiction in much the same way as addictive drugs.

Over the years, I have found two common foods that trigger or aggravate depression and anxiety in some people: dairy and wheat. It is absolutely amazing that when I put patients on a three-week detox diet, eliminating dairy, whole grains (especially wheat), and other common food sensitivities, many of their symptoms of depression and anxiety are totally resolved. Patients with depression and anxiety may benefit from blood tests that check for food allergies and/or sensitivities. For more information on this detox diet, please read my book *Getting Healthy Through Detox and Fasting.*

FOOD ALLERGIES AND SENSITIVITIES

Food allergies and sensitivities have also been linked to depression and anxiety. In addition to dairy and wheat, I have found in my practice that many people are either allergic or sensitive to eggs, corn, soybeans, and yeast—to name only a few of the most common allergens. Many times when a person is allergic or sensitive to a food, when they eat that food their pulse will increase. Dr. Coca, an allergist, discovered this decades ago. The greater the allergy or sensitivity, usually the greater the heart increases. This in turn can precipitate an anxiety or panic attack.

A BIBLE CURE *Health Tip*
The Coca Pulse Test

Perform the Coca Pulse Test. Take your pulse for one minute prior to eating. Then place a bite of the food to which you might be allergic on your tongue. After thirty seconds, recheck your pulse. If the pulse rate goes up over six beats per minute you may be sensitive or allergic to the food. The higher the pulse goes up, usually the more severe the allergy or sensitivity.

If you happen to be allergic to wheat, you also may be allergic or sensitive to oats. This allergy or sensitivity can lead to fatigue, depression, and anxiety.

If you are experiencing depression or anxiety and also have food allergies or sensitivities, I believe that it is critically important to desensitize from these foods (or in other words, to no longer be sensitive to them) in order to help relieve some cases of depression or anxiety. One of the best methods I have found is NAET, which is a form of allergy desensitization using acupressure. I have seen hundreds of patients desensitized from food allergies and sensitivities by using this technique.

If you have food allergies or sensitivities, I recommend that you decrease or eliminate from your diet all processed starches such as white bread, white flour, white rice, sugar, pastries, packaged foods, and potato chips. Increase your intake of vegetables, lean meats, brown rice, millet bread, and good fats such as flaxseed oil, extra-virgin olive oil, almonds, walnuts, and fish oil. Drink at least 2–3 quarts of alkaline water a day and follow my "Candida Diet" in *The Bible Cure for Candida and Yeast Infections*.

FOOD ADDITIVES

Food additives are a long list of chemical substances that are added to your food for flavor and color, to make it last longer, and for a host of other reasons. The largest group of food additives is the flavorings. Most of these flavoring agents are synthetic versions made from chemicals. Chemical food additives are usually made from petroleum or coal by-products.

MSG (monosodium glutamate) is a common food additive and flavor enhancer found in many processed foods, including soups, gravies, salad dressings, bouillon products, soy sauce, processed meats, ice cream, and so forth. It is also commonly found in restaurant foods, including most fried chicken products, sausage, scrambled egg mix, and grilled chicken fillets.

A new condition associated with MSG is excitotoxicity, in which the glutamic acid present in MSG can be neurotoxic by damaging and eventually destroying neurons by exciting them to death. I have found that it can also cause symptoms of depression and anxiety.

Another excitotoxin is the sugar substitute aspartame. When aspartame is broken down in the digestive tract, 40 percent of the final product is aspartic acid, another excitotoxin. This excitotoxin also overstimulates or excites nerve cells and may eventually cause permanent damage to the nervous system. Side effects of aspartame include depression, visual problems, headaches, confusion, dizziness, convulsions, brain tumors, and so on.

I have found that many food additives, and especially MSG and aspartame, can worsen the symptoms of depression and anxiety.

CHOOSE A HEALTHY DIET

Maintain a balanced diet, which includes lots of fruits, vegetables, whole grains, nuts, seeds, and lean meats. It also includes avoiding or dramatically decreasing your intake of the following:

- High-sugar foods such as sodas, desserts, cakes, pies, cookies, candies, and cereals

- Processed foods such as bagels, white bread, pretzels, chips, white noodles, and the white flour that much of these things are made from (even white rice is a processed food)

- Alcohol, cigarette smoke, and caffeine

The Seven Pillars of Health and *Eat This and Live!* discuss in detail how to maintain a balanced diet.

> You will keep in perfect peace all who trust in you, whose thoughts are fixed on you!
>
> —ISAIAH 26:3

A **BIBLE CURE** *Health Fact*
Excessive Caffeine and Sugar

Although coffee has many health benefits such as preventing diabetes and Alzheimer's disease, excessive coffee intake can worsen insomnia, depression, and anxiety. Excessive sugar intake has also been linked to depression. Most Americans drink carbonated beverages that are high in sugar and caffeine. Excessive caffeine and sugar intake will eventually lead to a loss in B vitamins, an increase in the stress hormone cortisol, and sleep disturbances. These nutrient deficiencies, along with an excess of cortisol and inadequate sleep, can eventually lead to depression and anxiety. If you do drink coffee for its other health benefits, remember that moderation is the key. Limit your consumption, and use a natural sugar substitute such as stevia.

THE BENEFITS OF TEA

A beverage that seems to be very important in mood disorders is green tea. Green tea is second only to water as the most consumed beverage in the entire world.[2] Green tea has been part of the Japanese culture for thousands of years.

Green tea contains many beneficial nutrients; however, one ingredient, L-theanine, is a unique amino acid that usually helps one to relax. In 1964 Japan approved L-theanine's use in all foods except for baby food. Even many Japanese soft drinks, as well as chewing gums, contain theanine. I will be discussing theanine in detail in chapter 5 as I talk about supplements to help relieve anxiety.

Years ago, a Finnish study of a large general population sample found that there was an inverse relationship between daily tea drinking (regardless of what kind of tea it was) and the risk of being depressed. They found that none of those whose daily tea intake was five cups or more had depression.[3]

Green tea is relatively low in caffeine content when compared to other teas and caffeinated beverage options. Since excessive caffeine should be avoided because it can contribute to insomnia, depression, and anxiety, please keep the following caffeine levels of various beverages in mind. I recommend sticking to green, white, oolong, or black teas while you are trying to overcome depression and anxiety.

CAFFEINE CONTENT COMPARISONS[4]

Beverage	Caffeine Content
Coffee (5 oz. cup)	16 mg/oz.
Black tea (one tea bag in 8 oz. water)	5 mg/oz.
Cola (12 oz. can)	3.75 mg/oz.
Oolong tea (one tea bag in 8 oz. water)	3.75 mg/oz.
Green tea (one tea bag in 8 oz. water)	2.5 mg/oz.
White tea (one tea bag in 8 oz. water)	2 mg/oz.
Decaf tea (one tea bag in 8 oz. water)	0.5 mg/oz.
Herbal tea (one tea bag in 8 oz. water)	0 mg/oz.

Dietary Fat and Depression

Years ago, scientists realized there was a link between omega-3 fats and mood when they noticed that populations who consume the most seafood have the lowest rates of depression. Scientists also found that low levels of omega-3 fats may correlate with an increased risk of suicide. Omega-3 fat supplementation has also been shown to be highly beneficial in those with bipolar disorder. Studies over the years have revealed that depressed people generally have lower levels of omega-3 fatty acids compared with omega-6 fatty acids.[5]

But not all fats are created equal. I like to group fats into three categories: beneficial fats, toxic fats, and fats that are allowable in moderation. I discuss this topic in detail in *The Seven Pillars of Health*, but let's look at each of these fats.

Beneficial fats

Beneficial fats that can help prevent the development of depression include omega-3 fatty acid. More than 60 percent of the human brain consists of fat, and approximately one-third of the brain's fat is composed of these beneficial omega-3 fatty acids.

Omega-3s create strong cell membranes. For nerve cells to function properly, the brain must have healthy, well-functioning cell membranes. This will directly influence neurotransmitter synthesis and affect levels of serotonin and other neurotransmitters. Serotonin levels are directly related to your mood; I will explain how this works later in this chapter. For now, understand that omega-3s are a key to fighting depression and anxiety.

As you may be aware, these beneficial fatty acids are found primarily in fish. However, I recommend using caution with regular consumption of fish, since it is being contaminated more and more with toxins such as mercury and PCBs. Fish that are still acceptable for consumption once or twice a week include wild Alaskan or Pacific salmon, mahimahi, sardines, rainbow trout, and tongol tuna.

A **BIBLE CURE** *Health Tip*

Although I do not recommend eating everything on this list, below are fish that have the least mercury content:

Anchovy	Perch (ocean)
Butterfish	Plaice
Catfish	Pollock
Clam	Salmon (canned; fresh)
Crab (domestic)	Sardine
Crawfish/Crayfish	Scallop
Croaker (Atlantic)	Shad (American)
Flounder	Shrimp
Haddock (Atlantic)	Sole (Pacific)
Hake	Squid (calamari)
Herring	Tilapia
Mackerel (N. Atlantic)	Trout (freshwater)
Mullet	Whitefish
Oyster	Whiting

Another great dietary source of omega-3 fatty acids is flaxseeds. Grinding the flaxseed makes it easy to consume in a number of different ways: eating it by the spoonful; mixing it into cereals or fruit shakes; or adding it to the ground meal of muffins, breads, and other baked goods. You can replace a few tablespoons of flour in your recipes with ground flaxseed without noticeably changing the taste or texture of your baked goods.

However, don't use flaxseed oil for cooking! Cooking with flaxseed oil oxidizes the oil and forms a very dangerous fat. I throw the bottle out after a month since it is very prone to oxidation after it has been opened.

I've mentioned dietary sources of omega-3 fats; however, most humans only convert a very small amount of flaxseed oil into EPA and DHA, which are the most important omega-3 fats in supporting brain health and decreasing inflammation. These fats actually improve neurotransmitter receptor sites (where they bind in the brain) by making the receptors more flexible. Low DHA levels are linked to low brain serotonin levels, which are related to an increased risk of depression, anxiety, and suicide.

Because it is so difficult for our bodies to convert omega-3 fats from foods into EPA and DHA, coupled with the fact that most fish are becoming more and more contaminated with pesticides, I commonly recommend pharmaceutical-grade fish oil supplements in place of eating fish on a regular basis. (See Appendix B for fish oil [omega-3] supplements I recommend.)

I believe it is extremely important to put children—even young children—on EPA and DHA supplements because EPA and DHA are essential for healthy brain development. Research also shows that supplementation with high-dose EPA and DHA concentrates can significantly improve the behavior of children with ADHD.[6] Some infant formulas are now supplementing with these important fats for brain health. You can also buy EPA/DHA supplements and follow the appropriate dosage instructions for children.

The average intake of EPA/DHA in North America is approximately 130 mg a day, but this is less than 40 percent of the 500 mg a day that is recommended by the American Heart Association in their 2010 Dietary Guidelines.[7]

Many physicians recommend doses of EPA/DHA of 1,000 mg to 2,000 mg a day of total omega-3 fats for our support for mood and brain health. However, some clinical studies that suggested that between 1,000 mg to 4,000 mg or more of omega-3 is needed to improve the mood in those with severe depression. I often prescribe between 1,000 mg and 4,000 mg to my patients, depending on what I am treating. (See Appendix B for more information.)

Toxic fats

Trans fatty acids or hydrogenated fats are toxic fats, which unfortunately are still being served in many restaurant foods and sold in many grocery stores throughout America. The good news is that processed food manufacturers now have to include on their food label the amount of trans fats in the food.

The bad news, however, is that if the food contains 500 mg or less of trans fats per serving, it can be listed as zero on the food label. Realize that any amount of trans fats in the body is toxic to not only the body but also the brain.

It is critically important that you eliminate all trans fats from your diet. Otherwise, these toxic fats will eventually be absorbed into your brain, setting you up for depression and anxiety.

Fats allowed in moderation

To understand which fats need to be consumed in moderation, you first need to realize that the essential fatty acids are from two families: the omega-6 essential fatty acids and the omega-3 essential fatty acids. A healthy ratio of the omega-6 to omega-3 is about 4 to 1. However, the ratio of omega-6 to omega-3 in the standard American diet is closer to 20 to 1. When this ratio is out of balance, it sets the stage for inflammatory diseases such as arthritis, heart disease, allergies, skin diseases, and emotional diseases, including depression and anxiety. Maintaining this delicate ratio is why I say that omega-6s are fats that are needed in moderation in our diets. When we take in too much omega-6 fatty acids, we increase our risk of depression.

The problem is that the standard American diet is chock-full of omega-6 fatty acids. They are commonly found in salad dressings, cooking oils (corn oil, sunflower oil, safflower oil, cottonseed oil, soybean oil), and processed foods like potato chips.

In addition to having higher omega-6 content in our foods, we have lowered the amount of omega-3 content in our foods. When America went on the low-fat diet craze approximately twenty-five years ago, we threw out almost all fats—including even good omega-3 fats. Research has shown that coinciding with the low-fat diet craze was an increase in depression.[8]

SEROTONIN-BOOSTING SNACKS

Now that I've discussed the foods to avoid because they will worsen depression and anxiety, allow me to share some of the things you *can* eat to boost your serotonin and alleviate symptoms of depression and anxiety. Since maintaining a steady blood sugar level is a key to keeping your mood from fluctuating, snacking is important. Even if you eat three healthy meals a day, if you eat the wrong snacks, you set yourself up for trouble. You must choose the right snack at the right time.

To boost serotonin levels I recommend one or two snacks each day. About three hours after lunch, eat a mix of approximately 30–40 grams of a starchy whole-grain carbohydrate with less than 3 grams of fat and less than 3 grams of protein. Although this seems like a scarce amount of protein, this is because too much protein can interfere with serotonin production. If you are trying to lose weight, you can decrease the carbohydrate grams in your snack from 30–40 grams to 25–30 grams, and eventually to only 20–25 grams. These snacks should be eaten on an empty stomach in less than ten minutes, and can be eaten again an hour before dinner if needed. Keep in mind that it usually takes about thirty minutes for the serotonin effect to improve your mood. If you have weight problems, you can take either 5-HTP or L-tryptophan as described in the next chapter. You can also eat snacks that are 40 percent carbs, 30 percent protein, and 30 percent fat that are listed in my upcoming book *Dr. Colbert's "I Can Do This" Diet.*

A **BIBLE CURE** *Health Tip*
Brain-boosting Snacks

Any of these snacks will jump-start your brain's serotonin levels. (These snacks help to raise serotonin levels in the brain.)

- Fiber One Oats and Chocolate Chewy Bar
- Fiber One Oats and Peanut Butter Chewy Bar
- Fat-free pretzels (one and a half ounces)
- Rice cakes, regular size (four pieces)

Once you figure out the snack that works best for you, I recommend that you put the amount equal to 30–40 grams of the snack in a resealable plastic bag. Then carry the bag with you in your car, purse, or briefcase. By eating these snacks at the specified times, along with healthy meals that consist of fruits, vegetables, whole grains, good fats, and lean meats, you will not only boost your serotonin levels, but you'll also alleviate your cravings for unhealthy snacks and comfort foods (like a whole tub of Ben & Jerry's ice cream). Do not choose a snack that you find irresistible and will overeat.

We have explored how proper nutrition can help us move from depression to joy-filled living. As you determine to eat right, pray for the strength to choose the right foods.

A **BIBLE CURE** Prayer for You

Almighty God, empower me spiritually to take control over my appetite so that what I eat helps my body overcome depression. Remove from me the desire for foods and thoughts that fuel depression. Fill me with Your Spirit so that I may discern and decide to eat and think right so that Your Spirit of joy will replace any spiritual heaviness in me. Amen.

A **BIBLE CURE** *Prescription*

Your Diet to Overcome Depression

In this chapter we have discovered that certain foods can help us overcome depression. Make a short list of foods you will begin including regularly in your diet:

_____

_____

_____

What type of tea will you choose to begin drinking, and how many cups a day will you drink?

_____

_____

_____

Describe how you will begin to limit sugar intake:

_____

_____

_____

Describe how you will begin to limit fat intake:

_____

_____

_____

JOY-FILLED LIVING WITH NUTRITIONAL SUPPLEMENTATION

G OD HAS CREATED wonderful natural substances that can help you overcome depression: vitamins, minerals, amino acids, and herbs. These powerful substances are readily available in health food stores. Although they are no substitute for consulting a physician or professional counseling, they will usually help you to overcome depression.

I've discovered that most people believe we get all the nutrients that we need from the standard American diet; however, this is simply not true. I find in my practice that nutritional deficiencies are quite common, especially in those with depression and anxiety. The standard American diet consists of fast food, sodas, junk foods, and processed foods that are usually very high in sugar and carbohydrates and low in fiber, vitamins, and minerals. These junk foods deplete our bodies of certain vitamins and minerals.

NUTRIENT DEFICIENCIES

Three specific nutrient deficiencies have been associated with depression and anxiety: the B vitamins, magnesium, and chromium. I believe that in order to alleviate both depression and anxiety, it is important to take a good comprehensive multivitamin that contains the B vitamins, magnesium, and chromium that will enable your body to make the necessary neurotransmitters, or "feel-good chemicals," to begin to change your mood. A comprehensive multivitamin and omega-3 fatty acid supplement, along with a healthy diet, provide the foundation for changing your mood. Let me discuss each nutrient briefly and then give you my specific recommendations for supplementing.

The B vitamin family

There are eight essential B vitamins, and these are important in patients who have depression and anxiety. Vitamin B_6 is extremely important in patients with depression and anxiety because it is critical to the synthesis of the neurotransmitters serotonin and dopamine.

Elevated levels of the amino acid homocysteine increase the risk of depression. However, three B vitamins—B_6, B_{12}, and folic acid—generally lower the homocysteine levels. These B vitamins also function as "methyl donors," which are absolutely necessary for human neurotransmitters to function efficiently.

Researchers have found that depressed patients are commonly deficient in B_6, B_{12}, and folic acid. I have found that vitamin B_6 levels are especially low in women on birth control pills. To insure you have adequate amounts of B_6, as well as the other important B vitamins, take approximately 800 mcg of folic acid, 500 mcg of B_{12}, and 2–10 mg of B_6. Good comprehensive multivitamins will contain adequate amounts of these important B vitamins. (Please see Appendix B for more information.)

Magnesium

Almost 70 percent of Americans are not consuming adequate amounts of magnesium in their diets.[1] Magnesium is very important for more than three hundred enzymatic reactions in the body. It also helps prevent muscle spasms, heart attacks, and restless legs syndrome, and it relaxes muscles. Magnesium may also help reduce nervousness and anxiety and may help you to sleep, especially if it is taken at bedtime. If you suffer from muscle spasms, eye twitches, jittery feelings, and anxiety, it is highly likely that you are not taking sufficient amounts of magnesium.

I typically recommend approximately 300–400 mg of magnesium a day; however, higher doses than this may cause diarrhea. Magnesium is found in seeds, nuts, dark green leafy vegetables, grains, and legumes. Good comprehensive multivitamins will usually contain adequate amounts of magnesium. (See Appendix B.)

Chromium

Chromium is an important mineral that helps to stabilize blood sugar levels as well as insulin levels. This in turn may help with mood swings triggered by hypoglycemia or low blood sugar. Again, realize that the standard American diet with fast foods, junk foods, and excessive sugars depletes this very important mineral from our bodies. I prescribe at least 200 mcg.

ANTIDEPRESSANTS VS. NATURAL SUPPLEMENTS

According to a recent study, the number of Americans taking antidepressants doubled from 1996 to 2005, with approximately 10 percent of Americans using these medications. Selective serotonin reuptake inhibitors (SSRIs) such as Prozac, Zoloft, and Paxil are the most commonly prescribed class of antidepressants.[2] Prozac and other SSRIs only prevent the reuptake of serotonin by the brain and do nothing about increasing the supply of other neurotransmitters. These drugs are also known to have side effects, which include suicide, loss or decrease of sex drive, nausea and vomiting, fatigue, anxiety, agitation, insomnia, diarrhea, headaches, sweating, tremors, skin rashes, and drowsiness.

Prozac and other antidepressants can also cause sexual dysfunction, including the inability to achieve or sustain an erection in men and the inability to achieve orgasm in both men and women.

Some newer drugs called serotonin and norepinephrine reuptake inhibitors (SNRIs), such as Effexor XR and Cymbalta, are also commonly prescribed, but again, I find that these have many undesirable side effects.

A BIBLE CURE *Health Tip*
The Truth About Psychotropic Drugs

For an eye-opening report on the disturbing reality of the antidepressant drug industry and what it is doing to our homes and families, I encourage you to get a copy of the documentary *Making a Killing*, produced by the Citizens Commission on Human Rights at www.cchr.org.

These are the main reasons I believe natural supplements are the better way to go in treating depression and anxiety. However, if you are on any of these medications, do not make any changes without first consulting your physician. Never just stop a psychotropic medication, but with the help of your doctor, begin to slowly wean off if it is recommended.

SUPPLEMENTS FOR DEPRESSION

Let's go over the natural supplement protocol I recommend specifically for arming yourself against depression.

SAM-e (S-adenosyl methionine)
SAM-e is the natural form of the amino acid methionine that has been sold as an antidepressant medication in Europe for more

than twenty years. SAM-e not only works as an antidepressant with few or no side effects, but it also may improve cognitive function and is useful in treating osteoarthritis as well as liver disease.

Numerous studies have shown the efficacy of SAM-e in treating the symptoms of depression. SAM-e actually helps to raise the neurotransmitters serotonin, dopamine, and norepinephrine in the brain.

Many physicians, especially in Europe, believe that SAM-e is just as effective as standard antidepressant drugs in treating depression. In fact, in 2003, after the U.S. Department of Health and Human Services reviewed one hundred clinical trials on SAM-e, it concluded that SAM-e works as well as many prescription medications without the side effects.[3]

SAM-e must be taken on an empty stomach. I usually recommend starting on low doses of 200 mg twice a day on an empty stomach, and gradually working up to 400 mg to 800 mg twice a day on an empty stomach, usually about thirty minutes before meals. This supplement is somewhat expensive. Please take a multivitamin with adequate amounts of B_6, B_{12}, and folic acid to avoid elevated levels of the toxic amino acid homocysteine.

5-hydroxytryptophan (5-HTP) and L-tryptophan

The amino acid called 5-hydroxytryptophan (5-HTP) was discovered in the 1990s and is derived from the seed of the *griffonia simplicifolia* plant from Africa. Its processing does not involve fermentation, and the seed is a natural source. 5-hydroxytryptophan is produced in the body when the amino acid L-tryptophan combines with vitamin C.

L-tryptophan and 5-HTP help to restore the levels of the important neurotransmitter serotonin, which helps alleviate depression and anxiety by regulating mood, behavior, appetite, and sleep.

There are several reasons I feel 5-HTP is superior to L-tryptophan. Researchers have found that in clinical trials, approximately 70 percent of 5-HTP administered orally is absorbed directly into the bloodstream.[4] This means that 5-HTP tends to be absorbed better than L-tryptophan. This also means that it is not necessary to take as high a dose of 5-HTP as tryptophan since more of it is delivered to the brain. Also, 5-HTP is a step closer to the formation of serotonin than tryptophan. And lastly, 5-HTP is able to raise the level of all monoamine neurotransmitters, which include norepinephrine, epinephrine, dopamine, melatonin, and serotonin.

L-tryptophan and 5-HTP are also quite effective in treating depression, which is usually associated with low serotonin levels. The normal dose of 5-HTP is 50 mg three times a day with meals or 150 mg at bedtime. However, after a few weeks, you may increase the dose to 100 mg three times a day with meals or 300 mg at bedtime. You should not take 5-HTP with any other antidepressants, such as Prozac, Zoloft, and Paxil.

L-tryptophan usually comes in a 500-mg dose. I usually recommend taking two to three capsules at bedtime. I recommend USP pharmaceutical grade, especially with L-tryptophan since the Centers for Disease Control and Prevention (CDC) linked a contaminated batch of L-tryptophan to a rare blood disorder called eosinophilia-myalgia syndrome (EMS), which was responsible for multiple deaths in 1989. It was taken off the market for a while, but has since been reapproved for use. Do not take both L-tryptophan and 5-HTP except under the supervision of a physician. It usually takes about three to four weeks to feel the benefits of these powerful amino acids.

A **BIBLE CURE** Health Fact

Caution About SSRIs and MAO-Inhibitors

WARNING! Be careful if you are taking SSRI medications with either 5-HTP or tryptophan. There is a condition known as serotonin syndrome, characterized by restlessness, tremors and shivering, agitation, confusion, delirium, rapid heartbeat, diaphoresis, hyperreflexia, blood pressure fluctuations, and myoclonus. You are more prone to serotonin syndrome if you take an MAO-inhibitor drug with either 5-HTP or L-tryptophan, or if you are taking an SSRI medication with high doses of either 5-HTP or L-tryptophan. For this reason, please consult with your medical practitioner before taking 5-HTP or L-tryptophan if you are taking an SSRI medication, and do not take either 5-HTP or L-tryptophan if you are taking an MAO-inhibitor.

L-tyrosine

L-tyrosine is an amino acid that is eventually converted to dopamine, norepinephrine, and epinephrine, which are neurotransmitters. Over the years, I have found that higher doses of L-tyrosine are fairly effective in treating some cases of depression.

I usually start patients on L-tyrosine at 500 mg, thirty minutes before breakfast and thirty minutes before lunch. I gradually increase the dose and find that 1,000 mg to 1,500 mg of L-tyrosine twice a day, thirty minutes before breakfast and lunch, is usually effective for many individuals with depression.

Be sure and take 10 mg of vitamin B_6 after taking L-tyrosine. Also, some people taking L-tyrosine benefit from taking an additional 500–1,000 mcg a day of sublingual B_{12}.

D,L-phenylalanine is another amino acid that is converted to tyrosine and leads to the production of neurotransmitters. Both tyrosine and phenylalanine have mood-elevating properties and may be beneficial along with 5-HTP. The dose of D,L-phenylalanine is two 500-mg capsules in the morning on an empty stomach and one 500-mg capsule later in the afternoon on an empty stomach.

St. John's wort

St. John's wort is an herb that has been used for centuries to treat both depression and anxiety, with its medicinal uses first recorded in ancient Greece.

An analysis of thirty-seven clinical trials concluded that St. John's wort may only provide minimal beneficial effects on *major* depression; the clinical trials also found that St. John's wort may be of greater benefit for people with *minor* depression. The National Center for Complementary and Alternative Medicine (NCCAM) and the National Institute of Health (NIH), cofunders of one of these clinical trials, found that St. John's wort was no more effective than a placebo when treating major depression of moderate severity.[5]

Therefore, I do not recommend St. John's wort for major depression. However, for mild depression or dysthymia, I usually recommend 300 mg of St. John's wort, three times a day. If this is not effective after about three to four weeks, I usually have my patients double it to 600 mg, three times a day. If patients do not see any benefits after two months, it probably will not help the depression. I must caution you not to take St. John's wort with any other antidepressants.

SUPPLEMENTS FOR ANXIETY

Now, I'd like to discuss a natural supplement protocol I recommend specifically for arming yourself against anxiety.

L-theanine

L-theanine is a unique amino acid that produces a relaxation effect on the brain similar to a mild tranquilizer. L-theanine is found in black tea, but higher concentrations are generally found in green tea—and the higher the quality of green tea, the higher the concentration of L-theanine.

> All praise to the God, the Father of our Lord Jesus Christ. God is our merciful Father and the source of all comfort. He comforts us in all our troubles so that we can comfort others. When they are troubled, we will be able to give them the same comfort God has given us.
>
> —2 Corinthians 1:3–4

A double-blind, placebo-controlled study of L-theanine in 2004 compared theanine with Xanax. Sixteen volunteers took either 1 mg of Xanax or 200 mg of theanine or placebo. Theanine, not the Xanax or placebo, induced relaxing effects that were evident at the initial measurement of whether a person felt tranquil versus troubled. Realize that 1 mg of Xanax is a significant dose, and most people use just 0.25 mg to 0.5 mg of Xanax.[6]

So, how does it work? Individuals experiencing anxiety, panic attacks, and insomnia usually have low levels of gamma-amino butyric acid (GABA), an amino acid I will discuss next. Theanine actually helps to produce a calming effect by boosting these GABA levels while it helps to improve the mood by increasing levels of serotonin and dopamine.

In patients with anxiety, generalized anxiety disorder, and other anxiety disorders, I generally recommend about 200 mg of

L-theanine one to three times a day. Also, I will often combine L-theanine supplements with the amino acid GABA and with 10 mg of vitamin B_6.

L-theanine crosses the blood-brain barrier quite easily and does not cause drowsiness. However, because it does help people relax, I recommend taking L-theanine at bedtime and find that it is effective in treating people with insomnia.

GABA (gamma-amino butyric acid)

GABA is an amino acid that also actually functions as a neurotransmitter in the brain. Both GABA and L-theanine are two of my favorite supplements for helping to relieve anxiety, and they usually work very well together.

Psychiatrists use benzodiazepines such as Xanax, Ativan, and Valium to control anxiety symptoms, since these medications cross the blood-brain barrier and bind to GABA receptors in the brain, helping to alleviate anxiety. However, supplements of GABA and L-theanine have a brain-calming effect very similar to benzodiazepines without the addictive properties.

GABA generally works best when taken on an empty stomach about twenty or thirty minutes before a meal and taken only with water. I usually recommend 500–1,000 mg of GABA one to three times a day; many times I will combine it with L-theanine and 10 mg of vitamin B_6. However, individuals with severe anxiety may need even higher doses of GABA.

GABA also seems to work best with vitamin B_6, and that is why it is so important to take a daily comprehensive multivitamin containing at least 2–10 mg of vitamin B_6.

5-hydroxytryptophan (5-HTP) and L-tryptophan

For anxiety, I usually recommend 5-HTP at a dose of about 50 mg three times a day or 150 mg taken at bedtime. However, if you decide to take L-tryptophan, I recommend taking two to three 500-mg capsules before bedtime on an empty stomach, taken with a small glass of juice. The sugar in the juice actually helps to enable the L-tryptophan to cross the blood-brain barrier into the brain where it can produce serotonin. You may eventually need up to 3,000 mg at bedtime; however, most people do well with 1,000–1,500 mg at bedtime. It usually takes about three to four weeks to see significant results.

There are numerous reasons I feel 5-HTP is superior to L-tryptophan, which are listed under my protocol for depression.

A BIBLE CURE Health Fact

What Is Tryptophan?

Briefly, tryptophan is an essential amino acid found in protein. It is a precursor, or building block, of 5-HTP, which in turn is ultimately converted to serotonin. Protein foods such as milk and poultry are rich sources of tryptophan. A lack of tryptophan flowing into the brain can result in depression, increased sensitivity to pain, and wakefulness.[7]

Kava kava

Kava kava is an herb that has been prescribed in Europe for years to treat depression, anxiety, and insomnia with fairly good results. Kava is nonaddictive and does not decrease mental functioning like antianxiety drugs, including Xanax and Valium. Kava is normally taken in a dose of approximately 45 to 90 mg of kavalactones three times a day.

Kava has also been used in the South Pacific islands for at least two thousand years without any known cases of liver damage. However, in 2002, there were at least sixty-eight suspected cases of kava-linked liver toxicity, including nine liver failures that resulted six liver transplants and three deaths. This resulted in countries in Europe, Asia, and even North America banning the sales of all kava products. However, many of these cases of liver toxicity involved the use of hepatotoxic drugs and/or alcohol with kava.[8]

In the United States, the FDA has issued warnings but has not instituted a ban on kava supplements. For this reason, even though kava does typically help people with depression and anxiety, I urge you to exercise extreme caution when taking these supplements.

Kava should not be used in anyone who has any liver problems or anyone taking any other substances that may affect the liver, including Tylenol and alcohol. If you develop dark urine or yellow discoloration of the eyes, which are both symptoms of jaundice, you should stop using kava supplements immediately and see your doctor for a liver function test. I also recommend that if you do choose to try kava, have your liver functions checked prior to starting this supplement, a month after taking it, and every three to four months thereafter.

Lemon balm and valerian root

Lemon balm is an herb that has been used for years for relieving anxiety and insomnia. I recommend a dose of 300 mg of lemon balm twice a day to help with anxiety.

A recent double-blind, placebo-controlled trial of thirty subjects suffering from both insomnia and anxiety received 300 mg of lemon balm twice a day, for a total of 600 mg. After only fifteen days of treatment, the participants in this study who received the lemon balm reported a 49 percent decrease in their state of anxiety and a 72 percent decrease in anxiety-associated symptoms as well as a 39 percent decrease in insomnia.[9]

Lemon balm is usually used in combination with valerian root, an herb that has been used for thousands of years as a mild sedative. This is sold over the counter and usually helps individuals sleep, but it also may decrease anxiety especially when combined with lemon balm.

Valerian works similarly to a benzodiazepine medication, stimulating activity of GABA receptors in the brain. However, because of valerian's sedative properties, I do not recommend taking it during the day. It should only be taken at night.

TARGETED AMINO ACID THERAPY

Targeted amino acid therapy is a term used to describe the use of supplemental amino acids and other nutrients to help balance brain chemicals (neurotransmitters). It begins with a special urine test, which provides a reliable means of measuring neurotransmitter levels in the body, which is typically indicative of neurotransmitter levels in the brain. Then combinations of amino acids and other nutrients are administered to patients in order to balance these neurotransmitter levels. The urine is usually checked about three to four months later to see how the patient is responding to therapy.

Since their discovery in the early 1900s, amino acids have been used to treat depression and other issues related to neurotransmitter imbalances. Even though prescription medications are more and more commonly used to treat these conditions, amino acid therapy remains a wonderful alternative for people seeking natural methods of balancing their brain chemistry.

I have found that targeted amino acid therapy usually provides significant relief to those patients with depression and anxiety and rarely causes side effects. (See Appendix B for more information.)

DEPRESSION AND HORMONES

Hormone replacement therapy is usually highly effective in treating middle-age individuals with both depression and anxiety. Both anxiety and insomnia are usually linked to an imbalance of progesterone and estrogen in the body in middle-aged individuals. Estrogen has an excitatory effect on the brain, whereas progesterone has a calming effect upon the brain. In other words, progesterone counterbalances the effects of estrogen.

Many women in the premenopausal period are estrogen-dominant, which means their bodies are producing too much estrogen and not enough progesterone. As a result, they usually suffer from insomnia and seem to be more prone to anxiety. Numerous studies have found progesterone to have antianxiety effects, acting on the GABA receptors on the brain. (As you recall, GABA is an inhibitory neurotransmitter that helps with relaxation as well as sleep.)

> And I will give you a new heart, and I will put a new spirit in you. I will take out your stony, stubborn heart and give you a tender, responsive heart.
> —EZEKIEL 36:26

For years, I have been recommending bioidentical hormone therapy for my female patients who suffer from low hormone levels. Unfortunately, most physicians use the synthetic forms of hormones. An example is Provera, a progestin or synthetic form of progesterone, which actually is linked to weight gain, fluid retention, and depression. Realize that synthetic progesterone will not help depression; however, bioidentical progesterone, which is the same type of progesterone that a woman's ovaries produce, will usually help both insomnia and anxiety.

I encourage you to talk to your doctor or a physician trained in bioidentical hormone replacement about hormone therapy options. If your doctor is not open to the idea of natural bioidentical hormone replacement therapy, get a second opinion. (See Appendix B for help in finding a board-certified doctor who is knowledgeable in bioidentical hormone therapy.)

Progesterone

When female patients seek my advice for depression, anxiety, or insomnia, I typically start by checking hormone levels, especially on middle-aged females. If a woman has low progesterone levels and has problems sleeping, I will typically place her on 100 mg of progesterone in capsule form at bedtime. If she is not having insomnia but is having anxiety and her progesterone is low, I will typically place her on a bioidentical progesterone cream.

Estrogen

While progesterone has a calming effect, estrogen has an excitatory effect on the brain. Too *much* estrogen production, which is common in premenopause, will usually cause sleep disturbances and anxiety symptoms. Too *little* estrogen, which is common during menopause, is linked to depression. This is extremely important in treating perimenopausal and postmenopausal women.

Many women come to my practice being treated for depression and taking antidepressants such as Prozac. But in reality, all many have is a hormone imbalance. Over the years I have found that women with low estrogen experience significantly less depression when using bioidentical estrogen replacement therapy combined with bioidentical progesterone.

As with progesterone, I recommend bioidentical estrogen and

not synthetic forms such as Premarin. Bioidentical estrogen should be administered in a transdermal cream or a patch since oral estrogen is associated with numerous side effects, including weight gain, high blood pressure, high carbohydrate cravings, and gallstones. Oral estrogen also interferes with tryptophan metabolism and serotonin metabolism.

Testosterone

Low testosterone levels are commonly associated with depression in men, including younger men with low testosterone levels. Studies have shown that older men with lower free testosterone levels in their blood are more prone to have problems with depression.[10]

I have found that long-term high cortisol levels caused from long-term stress, chronic insomnia, depression, and anxiety may be associated with low testosterone levels even in younger men. I have had some men as young as their late twenties with very low testosterone levels, usually from chronic stress, insomnia, and depression. There is an inverse relationship with cortisol and testosterone. Typically when cortisol levels increase for a prolonged period of time, testosterone levels decrease.

Unfortunately, most doctors check only the *total* testosterone and not the *free* testosterone. The total testosterone blood test measures all of the testosterone in the blood. However, much of that testosterone is usually bound to sex hormone binding globulin (SHBG), making it inactive. Even if a person has normal levels of total testosterone, it is possible that the majority of this testosterone is bound or inactive; therefore the test results can be misleading. That is why it is more helpful to know how much of the unbound, active ("free") form of testosterone a person has.

> Don't be afraid, for I am with you. Don't be discouraged, for I am your God. I will strengthen you and help you. I will uphold you with my victorious right hand.
>
> —ISAIAH 41:10

For low testosterone, I prescribe testosterone transdermal cream, and I check the blood levels of total and free testosterone and adjust the dose until the levels are normal. I also place patients on a natural supplement that will protect their prostate. I regularly check PSA (prostate-specific antigen) levels since testosterone supplementation is contraindicative with prostate cancer. I also combine the testosterone cream with chrysin, an herb that helps prevent the conversion of testosterone to estrogen.

I rarely have to prescribe testosterone injections since I can usually get the patient's testosterone level to normal by using transdermal testosterone creams. I prefer the cream because I find that patients injecting themselves with testosterone tend to have more side effects.

Thyroid

Although not a sex hormone, low thyroid levels, especially low T-3 levels, can lead to depression. Hypothyroidism and borderline hypothyroidism (called subclinical hypothyroidism) are fairly common in my practice. I can usually spot hypothyroidism as soon as I see a patient because of distinct signs and symptoms. Puffiness in the face and body, swollen eyelids, fatigue, constipation, unexplained weight gain, a loss of the lateral eyebrows, and edema in the feet and ankles are common symptoms. If a patient's T-3 level is low and the patient has depression, I usually treat the depression with T-3 (liothyronine) or Armour Thyroid, which is a natural thyroid hormone replacement therapy. For more information, refer to *The Bible Cure for Thyroid Disorders*.

A BIBLE CURE Health Fact
Toxins May Lead to Depression

Our world is very toxic. We are exposed daily to toxins in our food, water, and air. Heavy metals such as lead, cadmium, mercury, arsenic, and aluminum are ingested daily in our food, water, and even in the air we breathe. Solvents such as isopropyl alcohol, benzene, formaldehyde, and cleaning materials are being absorbed through our skin and being stored in our fatty tissues. We also are exposed to pesticides and herbicides due to the produce and fatty foods that we eat on a daily basis. Pesticides are easily stored in fatty tissue.

On a daily basis, our bodies are accumulating a heavier and heavier toxic burden due to our constant exposure to these toxins. These toxins are stored in our fatty tissues, nervous system and brain tissue, bones, and organs. They create such a toxic burden that we eventually may develop fatigue and depression. (You can learn more about detoxification in my books *Toxic Relief* and *Get Healthy Through Detox and Fasting*.)

As you overcome depression with joy, use natural vitamins and supplements to help your body eliminate any symptoms of depression and anxiety. Before you take your vitamins and supplements, pray over them. In doing so, God's blessing and anointing can empower what is natural in a supernatural way to be even more effective in physically strengthening you.

A **BIBLE CURE** Prayer for You

Almighty God, Your Word says in Jeremiah 33:3, "Call to Me, and I will answer you, and show you great and mighty things, which you do not know" (NKJV). Thank You for showing me which supplements to take. Before I take them, I pray for Your Spirit to impart potency to them for helping me physically and emotionally. Fill my body, soul, and spirit with Your joy that no circumstance can rob. Amen.

A **BIBLE CURE** *Prescription*

Overcoming Depression and Anxiety With Nutritional Supplementation

Circle the vitamins, minerals, and supplements you take regularly, and underline those you plan to begin taking. This does not mean that you are supposed to take all the supplements listed on this page. You should start slowly with a multivitamin and omega-3 fat, and start with only one amino acid supplement. A nutritional doctor will also help direct you through targeted amino acid therapy.

A comprehensive multivitamin

Vitamin B$_6$

St. John's wort

Magnesium

Chromium

Omega-3 fish oil

B complex

SAM-e

5-HTP

L-trytophan

L-tyrosine

L-theanine

GABA

Kava kava

Lemon balm and valerian

JOY-FILLED LIVING WITH EXERCISE AND REST

EXERCISE IS THE absolute best natural antidepressant. Regular aerobic exercise or increased activity can improve symptoms of anxiety, depression, excessive stress, and insomnia. Some studies have found that regular aerobic exercise is as effective as an antidepressant medication.[1]

Research shows that it may take approximately thirty minutes of exercise a day, at least three to five days a week, to significantly improve symptoms of depression.[2] However, smaller amounts of exercise as low as ten to fifteen minutes at one time can improve your mood in the short term.

Two main reasons active individuals feel better are that regular exercise may raise levels of certain mood-enhancing neurotransmitters in the brain, and it also increases the production of endorphins, which help relieve stress, decreasing the stress hormone cortisol. Endorphins are morphine-like compounds that elevate your mood, enable you to sleep better, and decrease muscle tension.

The problem is that many patients who are depressed or anxious have a hard time getting out of the house, going to work, or even doing menial house chores. They wonder, "How can I possibly start an activity program or an exercise program?" They simply see that as adding one more burden or one more chore to their life.

In these cases I recommend starting immediately on either 5-

HTP, L-tyrosine, or SAM-e. Before starting a new exercise program, I also recommend that you see your doctor and get his clearance that you are healthy enough to start an exercise program. Call a friend or an accountability partner—an "accountabilibuddy"—whom you enjoy being around and find an activity that you enjoy doing.

You do not have go to the gym and work out with weights or walk on a boring treadmill. You may want to take walks through parks, your neighborhood, or wherever there is beautiful scenery. You may want to even try ballroom dancing or try watching your favorite TV program while on an elliptical machine.

> He gives power to the weak and strength to the powerless.
>
> —Isaiah 40:29

If you do not enjoy the exercise activity you are doing, chances are you will not stick to it. So find an exercise or activity that you do enjoy. Also, make sure that you set a reasonable goal; instead of exercising five to seven days a week, try exercising every other day or three times a week. Have a day in between in order to rest. Start out walking only five or ten minutes a day, and gradually increase the time as well as the pace as you are able to. Eventually work up to twenty to thirty minutes three to five times a week.

Do not see your exercise time as a burden or something you *should* do. Remember, eliminate "shoulds" from your vocabulary; think that it would be a good idea for your health to exercise on a regular basis. For more information on exercise, please refer to my book *The Seven Pillars of Health*.

A **BIBLE CURE** *Health Fact*

Finding Your Target Heart Rate Zone

I used to recommend purchasing a heart rate monitor or calculating your target heart rate zone by using a formula I provided, but most modern exercise equipment now has a heart rate monitor feature built in.

However, if you don't have access to such equipment, I have a very simple solution. To find your target heart rate zone, simply walk fast enough so that you can't sing and slow enough so that you can talk. If you are walking so fast that you can't carry on a conversation, slow down. But if you are walking so slow that you are able to sing, speed up. Also, find a buddy who is close to your fitness level. I have seen spouses walking in my neighborhood, and the husband is way ahead of the wife. The poor wife is huffing and puffing trying to catch up. This will add more stress to your life because exercise should be enjoyable and not a chore.

RESTORING ADRENAL FUNCTION

Chronic anxiety as well as depression is usually associated with high-cortisol levels. Cortisol is the stress hormone associated with chronic and unrelenting stress; it is also associated with insomnia, truncal obesity, decreased memory, hypertension, and osteoporosis, as well as a host of other diseases.

I commonly check the adrenal status of patients with both chronic depression and anxiety and then support their adrenal glands with nutrients and herbs in order to restore normal adrenal function. For more information on this important topic, please refer to my books *Stress Less* and *The Bible Cure for Stress*.

THE IMPORTANCE OF SLEEP

Insomnia is a common symptom of both depression and anxiety, and that's why restorative sleep is extremely important in overcoming both of these conditions. Restful sleep leads to improved immune function, improved mood, a more youthful appearance, improved stamina, improved mental function, and improved memory. Sleep deprivation leads to a decrease in immune function and sets the stage for a whole host of illnesses.

It is critically important that you get at least eight hours of good quality sleep in order to overcome both depression and anxiety—this is even true for elderly individuals. Elderly people can have trouble sleeping well at night because they do not have normal serotonin levels that younger individuals have. Approximately one out of three people have insomnia on a regular basis.

Chances are you either have problems falling asleep, staying asleep, or you wake up in the early morning and find it difficult to fall back to sleep. As a result, most people with depression and anxiety are tired and have little to no energy to exercise. Realize that the same supplements to treat depression and anxiety also help many people fall asleep. I discuss this very important topic in detail in *The New Bible Cure for Sleep Disorders* as well as *The Seven Pillars of Health*.

The first step in correcting insomnia is to maintain a diet that is free of caffeine, chocolate, and other stimulants, especially in the late afternoon and evening. Caffeine inhibits the effects of serotonin and melatonin in the brain and also activates both the nerves and muscles, getting the heart pumping faster.

Alcohol is another toxic chemical that prevents a good night's sleep. In addition, avoid exercising too late in the evening or near bedtime since this will stimulate instead of relax the body. Never watch action-packed movies before bedtime, since they too can get your adrenaline flowing.

RELAXATION TECHNIQUES

Especially for people with anxiety, it is important to learn how to relax. When you have a panic attack or your anxiety level creeps up, simply practice some abdominal deep-breathing exercises or progressive muscle relaxation to abort an anxiety or panic attack. Also, simply ten good belly laughs a day will usually relax your body and decrease anxiety significantly. Understand that all anxiety disorders are marked by muscle tension, and when you relax the muscles, you usually relieve anxiety. I discuss many relaxation techniques in my book *Stress Less*.

Before falling asleep, try the following:

- Read the Bible or a good book, or watch a funny movie or TV show. Laughter helps to relax the body. I prescribe ten belly laughs a day to all patients with depression or anxiety. Turn off the late night news, and do not watch action movies or adrenaline-pumping ball games before going to bed. Instead, record them for watching the next day.

- Practice relaxation techniques such as progressive relaxation at bedtime. Relax while lying in bed. Begin by flexing the toes for one to two seconds and then relaxing them. Then systematically flex and relax the muscles all the way up to your head.

- Enjoy a light snack, before bedtime, consisting of 40 percent carbohydrates, 30 percent protein, and 30 percent fat.

- Cut back on your fluid intake past 7:00 p.m., and empty your bladder before going to bed so you do not awaken in the middle of the night and then find it difficult to fall back asleep.

- If you have tried all the basic steps outlined above and still find it difficult to fall asleep, take 100–300 mg of 5-HTP approximately thirty minutes to an hour before retiring. You may also take valerian and passionflower in a dose of 300 mg each approximately an hour before bedtime. You might also try 1–6 mg of melatonin thirty minutes to an hour prior to bedtime; take the kind that dissolves in your mouth.

One more note: if you are extremely anxious, you should decrease any activities that create additional stress. The steps above will help you to relax, but I also recommend that you avoid volunteering for extra work and eliminate all unnecessary activities that cause stress.

PRESCRIBING THE PEACE OF GOD

In this chapter, we have focused on the importance of physical exercise and adequate rest. However, the Bible cure affirms the benefits of *both physical and spiritual exercise for our continuing health.* The Bible says, "Physical training is good, but training for godliness is much better, promising benefits in this life and in the life to come. This is a trustworthy saying, and everyone should accept it" (1 Tim. 4:8–9). As you exercise your faith, trusting God to remove pain, strengthen, and heal your body, you will boldly pray for your healing.

> So humble yourselves under the mighty power of
> God, and at the right time he will lift you up in honor.
> Give all your worries and cares to God, for he cares
> about you.
>
> —1 PETER 5:6–7

God's Word encourages us to "come boldly to the throne of our gracious God. There we will receive his mercy, and we will find grace to help us when we need it most" (Heb. 4:16).

You can boldly approach God's throne in prayer. How?

- Believe in faith, trusting God for your healing.
- Trust His promises to heal you. For example, "He [God] sent his word, and healed them, and delivered them from their destructions" (Ps. 107:20, KJV).
- Pray boldly for your healing, knowing that in His mercy and grace, God's will for you is to live in divine health.
- Ask God to give you rest and peace. Jesus said, "Come to me, all of you who are weary and carry heavy burdens, and I will give you rest. Take my yoke upon you. Let me teach you, because I am humble and gentle at heart, and you will find rest for your souls" (Matt. 11:28–29).

For every patient with depression and anxiety, I recommend a list of specific scriptures that deal with peace of mind. Realize that "God has not given us a spirit of fear, but of power and of love and of a sound mind" (2 Tim. 1:7, NKJV). You are actually *promised* a sound mind, which is the opposite of depression and anxiety. I have found that when my patients meditate on and confess scriptures on a daily basis, both depression and anxiety usually begin to subside. (See Appendix A for Scripture confessions for peace of mind.)

A **BIBLE CURE** *Prayer for You*

Almighty God, in the name of Jesus and through His shed blood, I boldly approach Your throne of grace and seek Your healing power and touch. I know that by Jesus's stripes I have been healed. I claim Your promise that You have forgiven all my sins and healed all my diseases. So I boldly stand on Your promises of healing, and I praise You for helping me to overcome depression with joy. In the name of Jesus, amen.

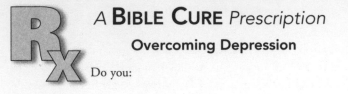

A **BIBLE CURE** *Prescription*

Overcoming Depression

Do you:

❏ Rarely exercise
❏ Exercise occasionally
❏ Exercise regularly

If you are not exercising regularly, when will you start? What exercise program will you implement?

_____

_____

_____

How many hours a night are you sleeping? How many should you be sleeping? If you are not getting enough sleep, what will you do about it?

_____

_____

_____

Check the steps you need to start taking before you fall asleep at night:

❏ Practice relaxation techniques
❏ Eat a light snack
❏ Other. Describe: _____

_____

_____

JOY-FILLED LIVING WITH THE WORD OF GOD

A s a physician, I am trained to carefully examine my patients and prescribe any medicines or lifestyle changes that may be necessary. I have found that my *most powerful prescription for healthy living* can't be found in a bottle or at a pharmacist's counter. It has one exclusive source, and it is freely available to everyone. I am talking about the Word of God, of course. Joy and peace can come to even the most troubled minds when people discover new ways of looking at life based upon the truth of God's wonderful Word.

Most depressed people have a very pessimistic attitude and are constantly beating themselves down with their thoughts, words, beliefs, and attitudes. Depressed people are usually in a pessimistic rut of negative thoughts that they cannot break out of on their own. That is why I believe it is absolutely essential for people battling depression to begin rewiring their negative thoughts with the Word of God. These biblical "self-talks" are extremely important in overcoming depression.

You may be asking, "How do I begin?" Begin to read scriptures aloud at least three times a day—before you eat your meals and at bedtime. Whenever a negative thought comes to mind, quote a scripture aloud to break the habit of negative thinking.

Throughout this book, I have inserted selected portions from the

Bible as your Bible cure verses for overcoming depression. Before falling asleep at night, repeat or pray these scriptures. Do so again when you awake.

> Those who have been ransomed by the LORD will return. They will enter Jerusalem singing, crowned with everlasting joy. Sorrow and mourning will disappear, and they will be filled with joy and gladness.
> —ISAIAH 51:11

One person I know has written these scriptures on three-by-five cards and put them in his pocket. Each day he pulls out his scripture cards and reads each scripture aloud to fill his mind with hope and joy.

WHEN SPIRITUAL WARFARE IS NEEDED

As I mentioned at the beginning of this book, certain symptoms of mental illness require treatment from a health care professional and simply cannot be addressed in a book like this. Likewise, when it comes to spiritual issues, there are certain spiritual conditions that can cause a person to become depressed or anxious, and they are much too serious for me to address in pages of this book.

The Bible speaks of a spirit of fear and other types of spirit beings that we must defeat through the authority of Christ. Some people can become victim to demonic oppression or possession, and situations like this fall beyond the scope of this book. If you think you may need to deal with this type of situation, I recommend that you seek the help of a qualified pastor or Christian counselor. I also recommend reading *Bondage Breaker* by Neil Anderson and *Dressed for Battle* by Rick Renner. I have also referred many patients over the years to Pastor Philip Fortenberry of Reconciliation Encounters, located at Cornerstone Church in San Antonio. (Please see Appendix B for more information.)

SPEAK UPLIFTING AND ENCOURAGING WORDS

You may not want to admit it, but you probably talk to yourself from time to time. Don't worry; it is very normal. In fact, the most important conversations that we have are those we have with ourselves! Unfortunately, people who are depressed tend to have mostly negative conversations with themselves. This makes things even worse because it means their minds are constantly barraged by nagging negative thoughts that beat them down a little lower each day.

I have seen fathers at Little League baseball games constantly criticizing their children, calling them stupid, dumb, pitiful—saying that they can't do anything right. I have seen the poor children standing in the outfield or slumped over sitting on the bench with dejected, depressed looks on their little faces. Unfortunately, some of these children who have been told that they are losers, that they are dumb, stupid, and can never do anything right, grow up to believe those words. They become depressed, unmotivated, and unsuccessful people.

If a person feeds on negative thoughts throughout the day, every task or every trial that comes his way will be approached from a defeated attitude before he even undertakes it. However, we have the ability, through the Word of God, to *speak* God's Word throughout the day and rewire these negative thoughts into positive thoughts, which will then bring healing and health to the body and the mind.

> The Spirit of the Sovereign LORD is upon me, for the LORD has anointed me to bring good news to the poor. He has sent me to comfort the brokenhearted and to proclaim that captives will be released and prisoners will be freed. He has sent me to tell those who mourn that the time of the LORD's favor has come, and with it, the day of God's anger against their enemies. To all who mourn in Israel, he will give a crown of beauty for ashes, a joyous blessing instead of mourning, festive praise instead of despair. In their righteousness, they will be like great oaks that the LORD has planted for his own glory.
>
> —ISAIAH 61:1–3

THINK JOYFUL THOUGHTS

As I mentioned in chapter 3, if you intend to overcome depression and anxiety, it is important for you to train your mind to think positive thoughts rather than dwelling on the negative. When a negative thought pops into your mind, it is important to cast down that thought and to speak out the solution, which is the Word of God. That is why memorizing and quoting scriptures is so important. Biblical, positive thoughts lead to winning attitudes.

An attitude is a choice. You can choose to have a negative attitude, or you can choose to have a positive attitude. You can choose to be angry, bitter, resentful, unforgiving, fearful, or ashamed. These negative attitudes eventually affect your health and allow diseases to take root in your body.

AVOID RESENTMENT AND UNFORGIVENESS

Resentment and unforgiveness are commonly associated with fibromyalgia and arthritis, whereas fear is commonly associated with cancer. Anxiety is commonly associated with ulcers, and anger is very commonly associated with heart disease. These are deadly emotions. If they are not taken out of us through the Word of God or with the help of a trained professional, they can eventually lead to disease.

When Paul and Silas were placed in prison, they prayed and sang praises (Acts 16:23–25). Paul had a choice. He could have had a negative attitude and become angry, resentful, and bitter. Instead, he chose to rejoice and sing praises. He chose the healthy attitude. He decided to "always be joyful" (1 Thess. 5:16).

When an individual wrongs you, it is very easy to hold bitterness, resentment, anger, and unforgiveness. However, this works against your body and will actually cause disease to set in. It is far better for your body—for both your mental and physical health—to forgive the person and release these deadly emotions before they take root in your mind, emotions, and body.

The Bible says it plainly: "Don't let the sun go down while you are still angry" (Eph. 4:26). This, I believe, is one of the most important keys in preventing these deadly emotions from locking onto our minds, emotions, and bodies and eventually killing us.

Paul decided to forget those things that were behind him and to press forward to the prize of the mark of the high calling in Christ Jesus. (See Philippians 3:14.) Choose the right attitude as soon as you wake up in the morning. When someone wrongs you, forgive that person immediately. Do not focus on the wrong.

SIX-MONTHS-TO-LIVE TEST

I like to tell people to take what I call the "six-months-to-live test." The philosophy is very similar to the Tim McGraw song "Live Like You Were Dying." I have treated a lot of patients with only six months or less to live. Many of these individuals have given up most of their distortional thought patterns, forgiven people whom they were angry with, and decided to live the remainder of their life in peace.

> Don't be dejected and sad, for the joy of the LORD is your strength!
> —NEHEMIAH 8:10

I also helped many of these patients forgive, accept, and love themselves. Most of these patients were tired of the world's treadmill of work, work, work. Instead of human beings, many had become "human doings"; many seemed almost relieved to be able to have an excuse to get off the world's treadmill.

Many people were able to reframe their thought patterns and to see people, circumstances, and even their disease from a different perspective. They gave up distortional thought patterns, hurts, bitterness, depression, and anxiety, and they forgave themselves and others and accepted and loved themselves and others. Some of them entered into sweet peace and joy, and some are still living years after they were only given six months to live.

THE POWER OF GRATITUDE

One of the most powerful treatments for both depression and anxiety is simply practicing gratitude; however, first it is critically important that you both identify and start reprogramming these distortional thought patterns as I described in chapter 3. If you did not read that chapter, please turn to it now. It is critical to do those two steps. Then you will be ready to practice gratitude, as I am about to describe.

In the past few years, there has been considerable research on living with a mind-set of gratitude. Researchers have found that gratitude helps you create a higher income, create superior work outcomes, experience a longer and better marriage, have more friends, have stronger social supports, have more energy, enjoy better overall physical health, develop a stronger immune system, have better cardiovascular health, lower your stress levels, and enjoy a longer life (up to ten years longer in one study).[1]

Research also proves that expressing gratitude makes everyone happier. Most people wrongly believe that happiness comes from what we buy, what we achieve, or where we go on vacation. That is simply not true; true happiness and joy come from within, and gratitude is a great way to gain access to this joy. Grateful people also sleep better, take better care themselves, eat a healthier diet, exercise more regularly, and have less depression and anxiety and more enthusiasm and optimism.

I love this quote from Melody Beattie:

> Gratitude unlocks the fullness of life. It turns what we have into enough, and more. It turns denial into acceptance, chaos to order, confusion to clarity. It can turn a meal into a feast, a house into a home, and a stranger into a friend. Gratitude makes sense of our past, brings peace for today, and creates a vision for tomorrow.[2]

One of the best examples of gratitude is the story of the ten lepers in Luke chapter 17. During the days of Jesus, the disease of leprosy was worse than AIDS. It usually started with disfiguring sores on the skin before advancing to nerve damage, fingers and toes falling off, and progressive disfigurement. It was also a very painful disease and, because there was no cure at that time, was actually a death sentence.

> He heals the brokenhearted and bandages their wounds.
>
> —PSALM 147:3

Once a person was identified as a leper, he or she was cast out of the city to live in a poor leper colony. A strict law stated that people could not even get within fifty yards of a leper because lepers were considered "unclean."

It was very rare to be healed of leprosy, but it did happen on rare occasions. To be allowed to leave the leper colony, a person was required to be examined by the priest and declared clean.

In Luke chapter 17 Jesus looked at the ten lepers and said, "Go show yourselves to the priest." On their way to the priest, they looked down and saw that their skin blotches were entirely gone and their leprosy was healed.

One of the lepers, a Samaritan, said, "Wait, I want to go back and thank Jesus." The other nine lepers were Jewish, but this one Samaritan leper (Samaritans were typically despised and treated as second-class citizens by most Jews) returned and threw himself down at Jesus's feet and thanked Him. Jesus then told the one leper to arise and go his way and that his faith had made him whole. Realize that *whole* means, according to Bible scholars, that missing body parts were restored. Why did Jesus do this? Because of the man's gratitude.

As in the case of the lepers, I believe that only about 10 percent (or less) of Christians practice gratitude on a regular basis. There-fore, there are just as many Christians suffering from depression and anxiety as the rest of the world. Think that over: 90 percent of Christians never stop and thank God for all their blessings

It's time to stop complaining about what you do not have and start thanking God for what you do have. I often recommend that my patients make a gratitude journal. It can be a fancy journal you purchase from the store or a simple three-ring binder or spiral notebook.

In this journal you will want to write something you are thankful for each and every day. Be sure to include various body parts and functions, such as your vision; hearing; the ability to taste, smell, and touch; the ability to walk and to use fingers, arms, legs, toes, back, and neck. Be grateful for every aspect of your health.

Also in your gratitude journal should be a list of family, friends, spouse, and other people God has brought into your life. Don't forget to be grateful for a hot shower, toilet, bed, refrigerator, stove, dishwasher, car, home, air conditioning, sufficient food, clothing, furniture, and so on.

Our thoughts lead to the words we say, and our words lead to our attitudes. We need to practice an attitude of gratitude. It is critically important to guard our thoughts and to quote the Word of God aloud throughout the day in order to produce godly attitudes within us. This is one of the most important points in preventing depression. Nutri-tion, exercise, and adequate sleep are all important. However, our thoughts, beliefs, words, and attitudes will determine if we succeed or if we fail; they determine where we spend our eternity as well.

You can overcome depression and anxiety with God's Word and by taking the various steps suggested throughout this book. *Don't quit. Don't give up.* God's hope and joy are available to fill you and defeat every spirit of heaviness in your life. Remember that your job is to keep your thoughts and intentions lined up with the Word of God, and He will be faithful to give you the joy and peace He has promised you in His Word.

> In every thing give thanks: for this is the will of God in Christ Jesus concerning you.
> —1 THESSALONIANS 5:18, KJV

I challenge you to take on a "can do" attitude, get rid of distortional thoughts, and believe in God's miracles and promises. Pray this Bible cure prayer as you overcome depression:

A **BIBLE CURE** Prayer for You

Heavenly Father, I know that You love and care for me. I pray that You will remove any spirit of heaviness from my life. Please clothe me with the garments of praise and joy.

Lord, help me to know which vitamins, supplements, and herbs to take that will help me fight depression. Give me rest and strength as I seek Your will in my life. Father God, remove the weight of grief, depression, and sadness from my life. Help me to remember Your Word as I seek wisdom and guidance in overcoming every aspect of depression in my life. I trust You, and I know that Your Word is true. Lord Jesus, You said that Your purpose was to give life in all its fullness. I thank You in advance for releasing this fullness in my life. In Your name I pray these things with thanksgiving and praise. Amen.

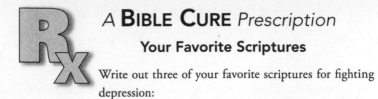

A **BIBLE CURE** Prescription

Your Favorite Scriptures

Write out three of your favorite scriptures for fighting depression:

_____

_____

_____

_____

_____

_____

_____

Circle one choice as to where you are, and place a check on the line where you need to be:

_____

Negative thinker   Positive thinker

_____

Resentful   Forgiving

A PERSONAL NOTE
From Don Colbert

GOD DESIRES TO heal you of disease. His Word is full of promises that confirm His love for you and His desire to give you His abundant life. His desire includes more than physical health for you; He wants to make you whole in your mind and spirit as well as through a personal relationship with His Son, Jesus Christ.

If you haven't met my best friend, Jesus, I would like to take this opportunity to introduce Him to you. It is very simple. If you are ready to let Him come into your life and become your best friend, all you need to do is sincerely pray this prayer:

> *Lord Jesus, I want to know You as my Savior and Lord. I believe You are the Son of God and that You died for my sins. I also believe You were raised from the dead and now sit at the right hand of the Father praying for me. I ask You to forgive me for my sins and change my heart so that I can be Your child and live with You eternally. Thank You for Your peace. Help me to walk with You so that I can begin to know You as my best friend and my Lord. Amen.*

If you have prayed this prayer, you have just made the most important decision of your life. I rejoice with you in your decision and your new relationship with Jesus. Please contact my publisher at pray4me@charismamedia.com so that we can send you some materials that will help you become established in your relationship with the Lord. We look forward to hearing from you.

CONFESSIONS FOR PEACE OF MIND

Scripture	My Confession
"Don't be dejected and sad, for the joy of the LORD is your strength!" (Neh. 8:10).	I refuse to be sad because the joy of the Lord is my strength.
"You will show me the way of life, granting me the joy of your presence and the pleasures of living with you forever" (Ps. 16:11).	I choose to stay in Your presence, and I am full of joy.
"The LORD is my strength and shield. I trust him with all my heart. He helps me, and my heart is filled with joy. I burst out in songs of thanksgiving" (Ps. 28:7).	I trust God. He gives me strength, and I am full of joy.
"He lifted me out of the pit of despair, out of the mud and the mire. He set my feet on solid ground and steadied me as I walked along. He has given me a new song to sing, a hymn of praise to our God. Many will see what he has done and be amazed. They will put their trust in the LORD" (Ps. 40:2–3).	I trust God and believe that He has put my feet on solid ground. I praise Him for the amazing things He has done.
"Enter his gates with thanksgiving; go into his courts with praise. Give thanks to him and praise his name" (Ps. 100:4).	I will always be thankful and full of gratitude for what Jesus has done for me.

Scripture	My Confession
"You will keep in perfect peace all who trust in you, all whose thoughts are fixed on you!" (Isa. 26:3).	I have perfect peace because my mind trusts God, His Word, and His promises.
"Surely He has borne our griefs and carried our sorrows" (Isa. 53:4, NKJV).	I give Jesus all my griefs and sorrows; I refuse to carry them anymore.
"To console those who mourn in Zion, to give them beauty for ashes, the oil of joy for mourning, the garment of praise for the spirit of heaviness" (Isa. 61:3, NKJV).	God gives me joy instead of mourning, the garment of praise instead of heaviness.
"Come to me, all of you who are weary and carry heavy burdens, and I will give you rest. Take my yoke upon you. Let me teach you, because I am humble and gentle at heart, and you will find rest for your souls" (Matt. 11:28–29).	I cast all of my burdens, worries, and anxiety upon You, God. In exchange, I accept Your rest and peace of mind.
"So now there is no condemnation for those who belong to Christ Jesus" (Rom. 8:1).	I have no condemnation; I cast down all condemning thoughts.
"For the weapons of our warfare are not carnal but mighty in God for pulling down strongholds, casting down arguments and every high thing that exalts itself against the knowledge of God, bringing every thought into captivity to the obedience of Christ" (2 Cor. 10:4–5, NKJV).	I choose to cast all worries and depressing thoughts out of my mind, and I choose to meditate only on God's promises.

Scripture	My Confession
"Don't worry about anything; instead, pray about everything. Tell God what you need, and thank him for all he has done. Then you will experience God's peace, which exceeds anything we can understand. His peace will guard your hearts and minds as you live in Christ Jesus" (Phil. 4:6–7).	I refuse to be anxious and worry; instead I will pray and confess God's promises and thank Him while in my circumstance. He will then give me peace of mind.
"Be thankful in all circumstances, for this is God's will for you who belong to Christ Jesus" (1 Thess. 5:18).	In all circumstances, good and bad, I'll give thanks and praise because it's God's will.
"For God has not given us a spirit of fear, but of power and of love and of a sound mind" (2 Tim. 1:7, NKJV).	I will not be afraid or worried. I accept God's promised gift of a sound mind.
"Give all your worries and cares to God, for he cares about you" (1 Pet. 5:7).	I'm giving all my worries and cares to God, and I refuse to worry.
"Such love [God's perfect love] has no fear, because perfect love expels all fear. If we are afraid, it is for fear of punishment, and this shows that we have not fully experienced his perfect love" (1 John 4:18).	God, You are love. I believe that as You live in me, Your love within me grows more perfect. I receive Your perfect love, and in doing so, I banish every trace of fear from my heart and mind.

RESOURCES FOR DEPRESSION AND ANXIETY

Divine Health nutritional products

1908 Boothe Circle; Longwood, FL 32750

Phone: (407) 331-7007

Web site: www.drcolbert.com

E-mail: info@drcolbert.com

Comprehensive multivitamin: Divine Health Multivitamin; Divine Health Living Multivitamin; Divine Health Multivitamin for Stress

Depression/anxiety: Divine Health 5-HTP; Divine Health Chelated Magnesium; GABA; L-theanine; L-tyrosine; Divine Health Living B_{12}; Divine Health Melatonin; Divine Health Relora; Divine Health Serotonin Max; Divine Health Stress Manager

Hormone health: Divine Health Natural Progesterone Cream

Omega oils: Divine Health Omega Pure; Divine Health Living Omega 3

From health food store

TryptoPure; SAM-e; St. John's wort

Spiritual warfare

Pastor Philip Fortenberry; Reconciliation Encounters

18755 Stone Oak Parkway; San Antonio, TX 78258

Phone: (210) 494-3900

E-mail: pfortenberry@sacornerstone.org

Bondage Breaker by Dr. Neil Anderson

Dressed for Battle by Dr. Rick Renner

Targeted amino acid therapy
NeuroScience
Phone: (888) 342-7272
Web site: www.neurorelief.com

WorldHealth.net
A global resource for antiaging medicine and to find a doctor that specializes in bioidentical hormone therapy

Food sensitivities
Sage Medical Laboratory
Phone: (877) SAGELAB
Web site: www.sagemedlab.com

Light therapy
SunBox Company
Phone: (800) 548-3968
Web site: www.sunbox.com

Thought field therapy
Callahan Techniques
Web site: www.rogercallahan.com

Cognitive-behavioral therapy
National Association of Cognitive-Behavioral Therapists
P. O. Box 2195; Weirton, WV 26062
Web site: www.nacbt.org

NOTES

CHAPTER 1: JOY INSTEAD OF SADNESS

1. R. C. Kessler, W. T. Chiu, O. Demler, and E. E. Walters, "Prevalence, Severity, and Comorbidity of Twelve-Month DSM-IV Disorders in the National Comorbidity Survey Replication (NCS-R)," *Archives of General Psychiatry* 62, no. 6 (June 2005): 617–627, referenced in The National Institute of Mental Health, "The Numbers Count: Mental Disorders in America," 2008, http://www.nimh.nih.gov/health/publications/the-numbers-count-mental-disorders-in-america/index.shtml (accessed July 8, 2009).

2. U.S. Census Bureau, "Population Estimates by Demographic Characteristics. Table 2: Annual Estimates of the Population by Selected Age Groups and Sex for the United States: April 1, 2000 to July 1, 2004 (NC-EST2004-02)," Population Division, U.S. Census Bureau, June 9, 2005, http://www.census.gov/popest/national/asrh/, referenced in The National Institute of Mental Health, "The Numbers Count: Mental Disorders in America."

3. J. R. Davidson and S. E. Meltzer-Brody, "The Underrecognition and Undertreatment of Depression: What Is the Breadth and Depth of the Problem?" *Journal of Clinical Psychiatry* 60, Suppl. 7 (1999): 4–9.

4. Adapted from materials created by the National Institute of Mental Health's Depression Awareness, Recognition and Treatment (D/ART) Program, Rockville, MD.

5. Kessler, Chiu, Demler, and Walters, "Prevalence, Severity, and Comorbidity of Twelve-Month DSM-IV Disorders in the National Comorbidity Survey Replication (NCS-R)."

6. Ibid.

7. World Health Organization, *The World Health Report 2004: Changing History*, "Annex Table 3: Burden of Disease in DALYs by Cause, Sex, and Mortality Stratum in WHO Regions, Estimates for 2002" (Geneva, Switzerland: World Health Organzation, 2004), referenced in The National Institute of Mental Health, "The Numbers Count: Mental Disorders in America."

8. Kessler, Chiu, Demler, and Walters, "Prevalence, Severity, and Comorbidity of Twelve-Month DSM-IV Disorders in the National Comorbidity Survey Replication (NCS-R)."

9. U.S. Census Bureau, "Population Estimates by Demographic Characteristics. Table 2: Annual Estimates of the Population by Selected Age Groups and Sex for the United States: April 1, 2000 to July 1, 2004 (NC-EST2004-02)."

10. Kessler, Chiu, Demler, and Walters, "Prevalence, Severity, and Comorbidity of Twelve-Month DSM-IV Disorders in the National Comorbidity Survey Replication (NCS-R)."

11. Belinda Rowland and Teresa G. Odle, "Depression," Healthline.com, http://www.healthline.com/galecontent/depression-1/5 (accessed July 10, 2009).

12. J. B. Overmier and M. E. P. Seligmann, "Effects of Inescapable Shock Upon Subsequent Escape and Avoidance Responding," *Journal of Comparative and Physiological Psychology* 64 (1967), 28–33.

13. J. Mendlewicz, ed. *Management of Depression With Monoamine Precursors* (n.p.: S. Karger Publishing, 1983).

14. R. C. Kessler, P. A. Berglund, O. Demler, R. Jin, and E. E. Walters, "Lifetime Prevalence and Age-of-Onset Distributions of DSM-IV Disorders in the National Comorbidity Survey Replication (NCS-R)," *Archives of General Psychiatry* 62, no. 6 (2005): 593–602, referenced in The National Institute of Mental Health, "The Numbers Count: Mental Disorders in America."

15. Carol E. Watkins, MD, "Depression in Children and Adolescents," Northern County Psychiatric Associates, http://www.ncpamd.com/cadepress.htm (accessed July 10, 2009).

16. R. E. Rector, K. A. Johnson, and L. R. Noyes, "Sexually Active Teenagers Are More Likely to Be Depressed and to Attempt Suicide," Washington DC: A report from the Heritage Center for Data Analysis, The Heritage Foundation, Publication CDA 03-04, June 2, 2005, referenced in Joe S. McIlhaney Jr., MD, and Freda McKissic Bush, MD, *Hooked: New Science on How Casual Sex Is Affecting Our Children* (Northfield Publishing: Chicago, 2008), 20.

17. National Alliance for the Mentally Ill, "Impaired Serotonin Activity Can Be Seen in People With Depression," August 21, 1996.

CHAPTER 2: PEACE INSTEAD OF ANXIETY

1. Kessler, Chiu, Demler, and Walters, "Prevalence, Severity, and Comorbidity of Twelve-Month DSM-IV Disorders in the National Comorbidity Survey Replication (NCS-R)."

2. National Mental Health Association, "Anxiety Disorders and Depression," Finding Hope and Help Fact Sheet, http://www.marquette.edu/counseling/files/anxiety.pdf (accessed July 10, 2009).

3. Kessler, Chiu, Demler, and Walters, "Prevalence, Severity, and Comorbidity of Twelve-Month DSM-IV Disorders in the National Comorbidity Survey Replication (NCS-R)."

4. Ibid.

5. Ibid.

6. Ibid.

7. Martin M. Antony, PhD, "Specific Phobia," http://www.anxietytreatment.ca/specificP.htm (accessed July 7, 2009).

8. Kessler, Chiu, Demler, and Walters, "Prevalence, Severity, and Comorbidity of Twelve-Month DSM-IV Disorders in the National Comorbidity Survey Replication (NCS-R)."

9. Ibid.

10. Ibid.

11. Roger Callahan, *Tapping the Healer Within* (Columbus, OH: McGraw-Hill, 2002). Quoted in *Publishers Weekly* review posted on Amazon.com, http://www.amazon.com/Tapping-Healer-Within-Thought-Field-Instantly/dp/0809298805 (accessed July 10, 2009).

CHAPTER 3: JOY-FILLED LIVING WITH NEW THOUGHT PATTERNS

1. David Yonggi Cho, *Fourth Dimensional Living in a Three Dimensional World* (Orlando, FL: Bridge-Logos, 2006) 30–31, 33.

2. Ibid., 55.

CHAPTER 4: JOY-FILLED LIVING WITH PROPER NUTRITION AND DIET

1. Charles Parker, "Celia Notes: Opiate Withdrawal from Gluten and Casein?" referenced in "Veggy Opiates—Stopping Milk and Wheat," http://www.happycow.net/forum/vegetarian/view_topic.php?id=218 (accessed August 13, 2009).

2. Yahoo! Green, "How to Green Your Coffee and Tea," http://green.yahoo.com/global-warming/treehugger-218/how-to-green-your-coffee-and-tea.html (accessed July 13, 2009).

3. J. Hintikka, T. Tolmunen, K. Honkalampi, et al., "Daily Tea Drinking Is
    Associated With a Low Level of Depressive Symptoms in the Finnish General
    Population," *European Journal of Epidemiology* 20, no. 4 (2005): 359–363,
    referenced in Terri Mitchell, "Natural Support for Sleep, Mood, and Weight,"
    Life Extension Magazine, January 2006, http://www.lef.org/magazine/
    mag2006/jan2006_report_theanine_02.htm (accessed July 13, 2009).

4. StashTea.com, "Caffeine Information on Tea," http://www.stashtea.com/
    caffeine.htm (accessed July 13, 2009).

5. Rich Maloof, "Omega-3 Fatty Acids," MSN Health and Fitness, http://
    health.msn.com/health-topics/high-blood-pressure/articlepage.aspx?cp
    -documentid=100135054# (accessed July 13, 2009); Carolin Small, "On
    Tenure Track: Joseph Hibbeln," *The NIH Catalyst*, May–June 2008, http://
    www.nih.gov/catalyst/2008/08.05.01/page10.html (accessed July 13, 2009).

6. Paul J. Sorgi, Edward M. Hallowell, Heather L. Hutchins, and Barry
    Scars, "Effects of an Open-Label Pilot Study With High-Dose EPA/DHA
    Concentrates on Plasma Phospholipids and Behavior in Children With
    Attention Deficit Hyperactivity Disorder," *Nutrition Journal* 6, no. 16
    (July 13, 2007), http://www.pubmedcentral.nih.gov/articlerender
    .fcgi?pmid=17629918 (accessed July 13, 2009).

7. American Heart Association, "2010 Dietary Guidelines," January 23, 2009,
    http://www.cnpp.usda.gov/Publications/DietaryGuidelines/2010/Meeting2/
    CommentAttachments/AHA-220e.pdf (accessed July 13, 2009).

8. Kristen A. Bruinsma and Douglas L. Taren, "Dieting, Essential Fatty Acid
    Intake, and Depression," *Nutrition Reviews* 58 (April 2000): 98–108, refer-
    enced in "Dieting and Depression," NaturalWellness.com, http://
    naturalwellness.com/catalog/dieting-depression.php (accessed July 13, 2009).

CHAPTER 5: JOY-FILLED LIVING WITH
NUTRITIONAL SUPPLEMENTATION

1. Dana E. King, Arch G. Mainous III, Mark E. Geesey, and Robert F.
    Woolson, "Dietary Magnesium and C-reactive Protein Levels," *Journal of the
    American College of Nutrition* 24, no. 3 (June 2005): 166–171, http://www
    .jacn.org/cgi/content/full/24/3/166 (accessed July 13, 2009).

2. Maggie Fox, "Antidepressant Use Doubles in U.S., Study Finds," Reuters
    .com, August 4, 2009, http://www.reuters.com/article/healthNews/
    idUSTRE5725E720090804 (accessed August 13, 2009).

3. Rowland and Odle, "Depression."

4. T. C. Birdsall, "5-Hydroxytryptophan: A Clinically-Effective Serotonin Precursor," *Alternative Medical Review* 3, no. 4 (August 1998): 271–280, abstract viewed at PubMed.gov, http://www.ncbi.nlm.nih.gov/pubmed/9727088 (accessed July 13, 2009).

5. National Center for Complementary and Alternative Medicine, "St. John's Wort and Depression," http://nccam.nih.gov/health/stjohnswort/sjw-and-depression.htm (accessed July 13, 2009).

6. K. Lu, M. A. Gray, C. Oliver, et al., "The Acute Effects of L-theanine in Comparison With Alprazolam on Anticipatory Anxiety in Humans," *Hum Psychopharmacol.* 19, no. 7 (October 2004): 457–465, referenced in Tiesha D. Johnson, RN, BSN, "Theanine vs. Xanax: Comparison of Effects," *Life Extension Magazine*, August 2007, http://www.lef.org/magazine/mag2007/aug2007_report_stress_anxiety_02.htm (accessed July 13, 2009).

7. Dean Wolfe Manders, "The FDA Ban of L-Tryptophan: Politics, Profits and Prozac," *Social Policy* 26, no. 2 (Winter 1995).

8. College of Tropical Agriculture and Human Resources, "Kava: Can New Research Findings Restore a Tarnished Image?" University of Hawaii at Manoa, May 2, 2003, http://www.ctahr.hawaii.edu/ctahr2001/CTAHRInAction/May_03/kava.asp (accessed July 13, 2009); Mark Blumenthal, "Kava Safety Questioned Due to Case Reports of Liver Toxicity," *HerbalGram* 55 (2002): 26–32, http://content.herbalgram.org/bodywise/herbalgram/articleview.asp?a=2147 (accessed July 13, 2009).

9. Stephen Daniells, "Berkem Builds Science to Support Anti-Stress Ingredient," NutraIngredients.com, March 22, 2007, http://www.nutraingredients.com/Research/Berkem-builds-science-to-support-anti-stress-ingredient (accessed July 13, 2009).

10. Osvaldo P. Almeida, Bu B. Yeap, Graeme J. Hankey, Konrad Jamrozik, and Leon Flicker, "Low Free Testosterone Concentration as a Potentially Treatable Cause of Depressive Symptoms in Older Men," *Archives of General Psychiatry* 65, no. 3 (March 2008), http://archpsyc.ama-assn.org/cgi/content/full/65/3/283 (accessed July 13, 2009).

CHAPTER 6: JOY-FILLED LIVING WITH EXERCISE AND REST

1. Andrea L. Dunn, Madhukar H. Trivedi, James B. Kampert, Camilla G. Clark, and Heather O. Chambliss, "The DOSE Study: A Clinical Trial to Examine Efficacy and Dose Response of Exercise as Treatment for Depression," *Controlled Clinical Trials* 23, no. 5 (October 2002): 584–603, abstract viewed at http://www.journals.elsevierhealth.com/periodicals/cct/article/PIIS019724560200226X/abstract (accessed August 13, 2009).

2. United Press International, "Study: Aerobic Exercise Fights Depression," RedOrbit.com, http://www.redorbit.com/news/health/122026/study_aerobic_exercise_fights_depression/index.html (accessed July 13, 2009).

CHAPTER 7: JOY-FILLED LIVING WITH THE WORD OF GOD

1. D. D. Danner, D. Snowden, and W. V. Friesen, "Positive Emotions in Early Life and Longevity: Findings From the Nun Study," *Journal of Personality and Social Psychology* 80 (2001): 804–813, referenced in Charles D. Kerns, "Counting Your Blessings Will Benefit Yourself and Your Organization," *Graziadio Business Report*, http://gbr.pepperdine.edu/064/gratitude.html#_edn7 (accessed July 14, 2009).

2. QuotationsBook.com, http://www.quotationsbook.com/quote/17764/ (accessed July 14, 2009).

Don Colbert, MD, was born in Tupelo, Mississippi. He attended Oral Roberts School of Medicine in Tulsa, Oklahoma, where he received a bachelor of science degree in biology in addition to his degree in medicine. Dr. Colbert completed his internship and residency with Florida Hospital in Orlando, Florida. He is board certified in family practice and anti-aging medicine and has received extensive training in nutritional medicine.

If you would like more
information about natural and
divine healing, or information about
Divine Health nutritional products,
you may contact Dr. Colbert at:

Don Colbert, MD

1908 Boothe Circle
Longwood, FL 32750
Telephone: 407-331-7007 (for ordering product only)

Dr. Colbert's Web site is
www.drcolbert.com.

Disclaimer: Dr. Colbert and the staff of Divine Health Wellness Center are prohibited from addressing a patient's medical condition by phone, facsimile, or e-mail. Please refer questions related to your medical condition to your own primary care physician.

YOU WANT TO BE HEALTHY. GOD WANTS YOU TO BE HEALTHY.

In each book of the Bible Cure series, you will find helpful alternative medical information together with uplifting and faith-building biblical truths.

The New Bible Cure for Heart Disease
The New Bible Cure for Cancer
The New Bible Cure for Depression & Anxiety
The New Bible Cure for Osteoporosis
The New Bible Cure for Sleep Disorders
The New Bible Cure for Diabetes
The Bible Cure for ADD and Hyperactivity
The Bible Cure for Allergies
The Bible Cure for Arthritis
The Bible Cure for Asthma
The Bible Cure for Autoimmune Diseases
The Bible Cure for Back Pain
The Bible Cure for Candida and Yeast Infections
The Bible Cure for Chronic Fatigue and Fibromyalgia
The Bible Cure for Colds and Flu

The Bible Cure for Headaches
The Bible Cure for Heartburn and Indigestion
The Bible Cure for Hepatitis C
The Bible Cure for High Blood Pressure
The Bible Cure for High Cholesterol
The Bible Cure for Irritable Bowel Syndrome
The Bible Cure for Memory Loss
The Bible Cure for Menopause
The Bible Cure Recipes for Overcoming Candida
The Bible Cure for PMS & Mood Swings
The Bible Cure for Prostate Disorders
The Bible Cure for Skin Disorders
The Bible Cure for Stress
The Bible Cure for Thyroid Disorder
The Bible Cure for Weight Loss & Muscle Gain

9418

PICK UP ANY OF THESE BOOKS IN THE BIBLE CURE SERIES AT YOUR LOCAL BOOKSTORE.